Edmund Burke

Twayne's English Authors Series

Sarah Smith, Editor

Tufts University

TEAS 286

EDMUND BURKE
(1729–1797)
Photograph courtesy of the New York
Public Library Picture Collection

Edmund Burke

By George Fasel

Twayne Publishers • *Boston*

Edmund Burke

George Fasel

Copyright © 1983 by G. K. Hall & Company
All Rights Reserved
Published by Twayne Publishers
A Division of G. K. Hall & Company
70 Lincoln Street
Boston, Massachusetts 02111

Book Production by Marne B. Sultz

Book Design by Barbara Anderson

Printed on permanent/durable acid-free
paper and bound in the United States of
America.

**Library of Congress Cataloging in
Publication Data**

Fasel, George W.
Edmund Burke.

(Twayne's English authors series ; TEAS 286)
Bibliography: p. 142
Includes index.
    1. Burke, Edmund, 1729–1797—Political science.
I. Title. II. Series.
JC176.B83F35   1983   320'.01'0924   83-8581
ISBN 0-8057-6861-0

For Katherine

Contents

About the Author

George Fasel took the Ph.D. in History and Humanities at Stanford University. He taught at Reed College, where he was Assistant to the President; the University of Missouri, where he acted as Director of the Honors College; and Upsala College, where he was Dean of the College. He authored *Europe in Upheaval: The Revolutions of 1848* (1970), *Modern Europe in the Making* (1974), and several articles and reviews in scholarly journals. George Fasel is currently Assistant Vice President, Corporate Communications, Bankers Trust Company, New York City. He lives in Manhattan with his wife

Preface

This book is intended as a brief introduction to the principal contours of Burke's thought and writing for those relatively unfamiliar with him and his age. It is not a biography or a systematic reading of every line Burke wrote. Rather, it is something like an encouragement to take up other books—most especially those written by Burke himself—to learn more about his life and thought.

Much of the subject matter here is political, since Burke spent the better part of his adult life attending to politics. There is attention to other matters, but the balance, I believe, is not unlike that one finds in Burke's collected writings. From Chapter 3 onward, I have kept the account chronological, with the exception of Chapter 4, where I have brought together his thoughts on overseas politics which were expressed during the course of a quarter century.

Parts of Chapters 5 and 6 appeared, in substantially different form, in *Studies in Burke and His Time* 17 (1976), whose permission to rework them here is gratefully acknowledged. Some of the research and writing were conducted thanks to the generosity of the National Endowment for the Humanities and the Research Council of the University of Missouri, in whose debt I stand. Rachel Vorspan, Donald N. Baker, and John F. H. New were kind enough to give an earlier version of the manuscript a helpful reading. Jean Ann Peters typed the manuscript cheerfully, under less than ideal conditions. The contribution of my wife, Katherine, is on every page—between the lines.

George Fasel

Chronology

1729 Burke born in Dublin.

1743 Enrolls in Trinity College, Dublin.

1750 Begins law studies at the Middle Temple, London.

1756 Marriage; publication of *A Vindication of Natural Society* and *A Philosophical Enquiry into the Origin of Our Ideas on the Sublime and Beautiful*.

1758 Birth of a son, Richard; begins to edit the *Annual Register*.

1759 Becomes private secretary to William Gerard Hamilton.

1765 Breaks with Hamilton; becomes private secretary to Marquis of Rockingham, who forms his first government; Burke elected to Parliament for Wendover (December).

1766 Enters Parliament; Rockingham government passes a Declaratory Act on the American colonies and repeals the Stamp Act of 1765 before dissolving in June.

1768 Purchases an estate for £20,000 in Buckinghamshire; John Wilkes elected for Middlesex.

1769 Publishes *Observations on a Late Publication, Intituled "The Present State of the Nation"*; Wilkes finally unseated by Parliament.

1770 Publishes *Thoughts on the Cause of the Present Discontents*; Lord North forms his government.

1773 Visits France.

1774 Delivers *Speech on American Taxation* (19 April); elected to Parliament for Bristol.

1775 Delivers *Speech on Conciliation with America* (22 March); war begins in America (April).

1777 Publishes *Letter to the Sheriffs of Bristol*.

1780   Submits to the House of Commons his proposal for "economical reform"; serious rioting in London; withdraws from campaign for reelection at Bristol, elected to Parliament for Malton.

1782   North's government succeeded by second Rockingham government, with Burke as Paymaster of the Forces; death of Rockingham.

1783   William Pitt the Younger forms his government.

1786   Burke moves the impeachment of Warren Hastings.

1787   Hastings impeached by the House of Commons.

1788   Hastings's trial begins in the House of Lords.

1789   Beginning of the French revolution: meeting of the Estates-General at Versailles (May); formation of the National Assembly (June); attack on the Bastille (July); peasant rioting in the countryside (July-August); popular invasion of the royal palace and forcible return of the royal family to Paris (October).

1790   Burke begins to move apart from certain Whigs on the question of the French revolution; publishes *Reflections on the Revolution in France* (November).

1791   Increasing rift among the Whigs; Burke publishes *An Appeal from the New to the Old Whigs* and *A Letter to a Member of the French National Assembly*; *Thoughts on French Affairs* written (December).

1792   France declares war on Austria and Prussia (April); French monarchy overthrown and replaced by a republic (August).

1793   Execution of Louis XVI; France declares war on England; beginning of the reign of terror in France.

1794   Burke retires from Parliament; his son Richard dies.

1795   Acquittal of Hastings by the House of Lords; *Thoughts and Details on Scarcity* (presented to Pitt in November).

1796   *A Letter to a Noble Lord.*

1796–1797   *Letters on a Regicide Peace.*

1797   Burke's death (9 July).

Chapter One
The Outsider

Sources for a biography of Edmund Burke become truly rich only in the second half of his life. We can speak with considerable confidence of the pertinent facts, and more, of his maturity—a condition which renders our ignorance about his youth and early manhood especially frustrating. Burke only comes alive for us, in rich human complexity, during his middle thirties; just how the earlier years made that man we must frequently speculate.

A Talent in Search of a Career

Burke was born in Dublin in 1729; his father was an attorney and a Protestant, his mother a Roman Catholic. Edmund attended a Quaker school, where he formed his closest youthful friendship with Richard Shackleton, the son of the headmaster. In 1744, he enrolled in Trinity College, Dublin, where he pursued an orthodox eighteenth-century tour through classical literature, his own tastes leaning toward poetry and history. Some letters to Shackleton survive from these years, but they are written from behind a persona of supercilious nonchalance toward his studies. In fact, Burke worked hard enough to win a scholarship while also finding time to help organize an undergraduate debating society.

The senior Burke was determined that Edmund would also follow a career in the law and in 1750 packed his son off to London for studies at the Middle Temple—at which point Edmund very nearly drops out of our sight for six years. We do know that he was keenly dissatisfied with his legal studies and that the pull of a literary career had begun to exert itself. In his Trinity days, Burke had sent Shackleton numerous rather limp attempts at verse, and was clearly eager for his approval. On one occasion, Burke referred to a mutual friend: "Don't you think had he money to bear his charges but 'twere his best course to go to London? I am told that a man who writes, can't miss there of getting some bread, and possibly good.

1

I heard the other day of a gentleman who maintained himself in the study of the law by writing pamphlets in favour of the ministry."[1] Roughly six months after arriving in London himself, Burke revealed in couplets how literature competed for his attention ("Full half his Laurels Richlieu would resign, / O Envied Corneille, for one Branch of thine").[2] Although this unpublished epistolary verse was entitled "The Muse Divorced," no such finality is apparent in the text.

Legal education at the time was scarcely designed to nurture aesthetic sensibilities. When Burke began his studies, it was still fifteen years before Blackstone would begin to publish his *Commentaries*; one read in tomes which were usually old, straitened, highly technical, and largely given over to various baffling permutations in the law of real property. Generally, it took seven years before a man could advance to the bar. Burke eventually lost patience, though exactly when is uncertain. In the early 1750s, we catch only glimpses of him—in poor health, and recovering under the ministrations of a physician whose daughter Burke would marry in 1757; exchanging verses and brief philosophical sketches with "cousin" Will Burke, now his closest friend (and with whom there may in fact have been no familial relationship); attempting to move from the periphery closer to the center of London literary life; living impecuniously, since his father—a man of no vast wealth in any event—was unenthusiastic about any career other than the law.

But if the extant records are maddeningly silent on these years, we must still conclude that Burke did not spend them in idleness or mental sloth. Indeed, by 1756 he had arrived—though we know not how—at certain intellectual positions to which he clung for the rest of his life. With little hint as to their derivation, they appeared that year in his first published work (beyond some contributions to an undergraduate newspaper), *A Vindication of Natural Society*.

Satire was a popular mode in the early eighteenth century, and in the Augustan twilight of 1756 Burke tried on the satirical voice to reveal the vast and destructive implications of certain political and religious attitudes. Some reviewers missed the point, as reviewers will, and took the attack for a defense. In a second printing the following year, Burke was forced to add a preface clarifying his intentions.

He had better luck in a second book, published the same year as the *Vindication*, a treatise on aesthetics which familiarized his name among some of the leading writers of the age. *A Philosophical Enquiry into the Origin of Our Ideas of the Sublime and Beautiful* touched on issues of physiology, psychology, and philosophy, but most notably it challenged the classical "objective" aesthetic head-on. Yet while the *Enquiry*, upon which he had apparently been at work since his Trinity days, reached a European audience, it failed to bring him anything like financial independence.[3]

Indeed, in spite of the impressive output of 1756, a career in literature was beginning to seem increasingly remote. The *Vindication* had received some notice, the *Enquiry* something approaching renown in bookish circles. Yet renown proved unnourishing, and by 1758 there was a son, Richard, to be cared for. Burke turned out some 90,000 words of *An Essay Toward an Abridgement of the English History*, but he could not get the story beyond the Magna Carta and it remained unpublished in his lifetime.[4] His publishers, the respectable Dodsley brothers, accepted his proposal to serve as the editor of a new magazine which would review the books and principal events of the preceding year. But the *Annual Register*, which first appeared in 1758, paid meagerly. Moreover, as a "journalistic" publication, its editorship brought uncomfortably low status; Burke never publicly acknowledged the connection.[5]

Well into the early 1760s, Burke held to hopes of a future in literature. In retrospect, however, it is clear that by 1759 he had begun to drift into politics. His financial situation desperate, he accepted employment as private secretary to William Gerard Hamilton, a Member of Parliament with aspirations to high office. Although Burke never looked upon the position as more than a stopgap and had clearly indicated to Hamilton that his literary ambitions would permit him no long-term commitments, still it afforded him valuable experience. It broadened his circle of acquaintances and gave him something like an insider's view of English politics.[6] In addition, Hamilton was eventually able to secure Burke a £300 annual pension.

In the meantime, however, Burke's connections remained primarily literary—most notably within that remarkable conversational society known simply as The Club, whose participants included at one time or another such luminaries as Dr. Samuel Johnson, Sir Joshua Reynolds, Adam Smith, Oliver Goldsmith, Edward Gibbon, and David Garrick. During the same period, Burke also began essays on the drama and on religious toleration in Ireland (neither of which he completed). In time, however, he began to fear that he had become tied to an employer more master than patron, that his own position was less subordinate than servile. As a result, he resigned his secretaryship in 1765—and with it, of course, his pension.

Plainly, it was a major gamble, and even after events proved that he had won it, Burke was not entirely convinced. He was, after all, thirty-six—hardly youthful by the measure of his time—hopeful of a life in literature but with little evidence to show that he could support himself and his family adequately by "respectable" writing, embarrassed to admit to the sort of work that brought him his only income. Without formally renouncing the ambitions of authorship, Burke seems finally to have concluded that his prospects were more promising in that area where he had accumulated six years' experience. In the spring of 1765, therefore, he began casting about for another political lieutenancy, preferably with a more prepossessing figure than Hamilton.

Opportunity presented itself in July, when the second Marquis of Rockingham hired Burke as his private secretary. Rockingham, a year junior to Burke, commanded vast wealth and mounting political influence; he was about to enter a new government as First Lord of the Treasury. Yet Burke felt that his "cousin" Will, who was about to be appointed to a more prestigious government position, had picked a larger plum, and Edmund wrote to a friend: "I have got an employment of a kind humble enough; but which may be worked into some sort of consideration, or at least advantage; Private Secretary to Lord Rockingham, who has the reputation of a man of honour and integrity; and with whom, they say, it is not difficult to live. Will is strongly talked of for a better thing."[7]

Will Burke's connections were indeed excellent. By the end of the year, he was preparing to enter Parliament through the good offices of a patron, Lord Verney, who controlled (among other things) the election to the seat for Wendover, in Buckinghamshire. But Will had always considered his own abilities inferior to Edmund's, and he persuaded Verney that the seat should go to his closest friend. Edmund accepted, with gratitude, but without much enthusiasm, if we can accept his account of some two years later:

Every body congratulated me on coming into the House of Commons, as being in the certain Road of a great and speedy fortune; and when I began to be heard with some little attention, every one of my friends was sanguine. But in truth I never was so myself. I came into Parliament not at all as a place of preferment, but of refuge; I was pushed into it; and I must have been a Member, and that too with some Eclat, or be a little worse than nothing. . . .But I considered my situation on the side of fortune as very precarious.[8]

The Political Vocation

The connection with Rockingham and the election to Parliament did not automatically guarantee Burke a long and successful political career. If anything, he faced substantial disadvantages. To begin with, he was Irish, with bright red hair and an accent which even with the passage of years was "as strong," in the words of one listener, "as if he had never quitted the banks of the Shannon. . . ."[9] The English subjection of Ireland had begun six centuries before Burke was born. By his own time, political, economic, social, and religious discrimination against the Irish—even against Protestants, such as Burke—was deeply ingrained in English behavior. Ambitious Irishmen were regarded in England with wary skepticism at best, and in certain circles Burke soon developed the reputation of an upstart, a climber, an "Irish adventurer." Moreover, his origins, and the fact that both his mother and the family of the Englishwoman he married were Roman Catholics, convinced some people that Burke was in reality a closet Papist.

There was also the fact that eighteenth-century English politics remained predominantly the preserve of landed wealth, of high social status, of noble titles or close family connections with them, of long-standing and almost habitual political influence. Burke possessed none of these attributes. It is true that in 1768 he purchased a six-hundred-acre estate in Buckinghamshire, thereby conferring on him some of the prestige connected with landownership. As a landed gentleman, he assumed a social stature which enabled him to view other members of Parliament from somewhere closer to eye level.[10] Even so, he was a member of the landed classes, but hardly of the landed elite, as he suggested in an arresting metaphor employed in a letter to the Duke of Richmond in 1772:

You people of great families and hereditary Trusts and fortunes are not like such as I am, who whatever we may be by the Rapidity of our growth and of the fruit we bear, flatter ourselves that while we creep on the Ground we belly into melons that are exquisite for size and flavour, yet

still we are but annual plants that perish with our Season and leave no
sort of Traces behind us. You if you are what you ought to be are the
great Oaks that shade a Country and perpetuate your benefits from Generation to Generation.[11]

Besides being Irish and a commoner of no impressive means,
Burke was also a Whig. The first two disabilities were enough to
keep him from high political office. The third very nearly kept him
from *all* political office, with one very brief exception, since Whig
governments were a rarity during George III's reign. Burke's political life was largely confined to the Opposition, not ordinarily a
place where brilliant careers are made.

Burke's disabilities were the accidents of birth, not the absence
of talent. Dr. Johnson said of him, "Yes, Sir, if a man were to go
by chance at the same time with Burke under a shed to shun a
shower, he would say—'This is an extraordinary man.' "[12] Burke
quickly proved himself an effective, if not universally popular, orator
in the House of Commons. In both his speeches and writings he
demonstrated an unusual ability to command massive bodies of facts
and figures. His knowledge of imperial affairs equaled that of domestic issues. He counted for enough to have important enemies.
Yet, to the end, he remained an outsider.

Even so, Burke responded to his circumstances only rarely with
rancor. To the contrary, he accepted most of the British political
system and virtually all the social system in which it was rooted;
in time, he became their most eloquent defender. Plainly the outsider approved of things on the inside.

When Burke entered Parliament, the major issues which were to
preoccupy him for the next quarter century were only beginning to
take shape. The accession of King George III in 1760 brought certain
political modulations which, although relatively minor in retrospect, occasioned considerable concern at the time. What now appear
to have been questions of advantage and influence seemed then to
have been freighted with constitutional significance. What actually
happened was that Whiggish elements which had largely dominated
government throughout the early eighteenth century were being
replaced by groups the new king found more congenial. Convinced
that these maneuverings carried more ominous implications, Burke
took on the role of spokesman for the Rockingham group in 1770
with his first major political pronouncement since joining the House

of Commons. *Thoughts on the Cause of the Present Discontents* prompted some stir upon its publication; more important, it has stood for two centuries as a major analysis of the British constitution, a pioneering exploration of the role of political parties, and a monument to Burke's prose style.

At the same time, the British empire—which had attained unprecedented vastness with the conquests of the Seven Years War (1756–63)—was becoming the source of serious difficulties. The North American colonies were proving increasingly refractory, and all efforts to bring them to heel either were ineffectual or exacerbated the problem. Although at bottom Burke wished to maintain the unity of the empire, still he was sensitive to the special circumstances of America, feelings which were probably heightened during his years of paid service as a colonial agent—that is, something like a lobbyist—for New York. As the fund of patience dwindled in Parliament and the likelihood of war mounted, Burke urged moderation, accommodation, and plain common sense upon his colleagues, to no avail. These efforts most notably produced the *Speech on American Taxation*, in 1774, and the *Speech on Conciliation with America*, a year later, arguments which failed to sway policy but broadened Burke's constitutional inquiries to a global scale.

During these same years, Burke gave up his parliamentary seat in tiny Wendover for one from the city of Bristol, a thriving western commercial port and thus one of the more conspicuous constituencies in the land. It was, almost from the beginning, a *mésalliance*. Burke's views on America ran counter to those of a heavily mercantile electorate which wished to keep the American markets in a pliable and exploitable status. Similarly, his repeated calls for a more lenient relationship with subject Ireland and for the relaxation of harsh anti-Catholic legislation aroused resentment in the same Bristol circles, long accustomed to enjoy the considerable advantages of trading with the subordinate Irish. Burke's constituents insisted that his votes reflect their preferences in such matters—surely a reasonable interpretation of representative government. Burke held that Bristol had elected his character and judgment, that he was morally bound to exercise these capacities on behalf of the entire realm rather than a single city, and that he must be left free to vote his convictions. It was an equally reasonable interpretation, but it also saddled Burke with an impossible dilemma. By 1780, he knew he could not resolve it, and withdrew from the election campaign of that year, seeking reelection instead in the safe seat for Malton.

Constitutional and imperial questions, and their frequent intersections, remained the focus of Burke's public career during the subsequent decade. In 1780, for example, he put forward the only noteworthy piece of legislation associated with his name during thirty years in the House of Commons. In a major speech proposing "economical reform," Burke sought once again to deal with the matter of royal influence by striking at its financial foundation in the power of patronage. But it was increasingly plain that his contributions were not to be as lawmaker, or even as governor—he attained his highest position in 1782, during a brief Rockingham ministry, as the not especially exalted Paymaster of the Forces. Assigned by circumstances to a career in opposition, Burke's strengths were those of a critic, a gadfly who called attention to excesses, a conscience determined to let no violation of constitutional principle go unnoticed.

Much of his energy in the 1780s was poured into this role, especially with respect to the empire. When certain irregularities in the British rule of India came to his notice, he launched extensive investigations and was finally persuaded that the obligations of fair and responsible governance had been breached. In time, his ire centered on Warren Hastings, the British Governor General in India, whose impeachment Burke put before the House of Commons in 1786 and achieved—after massive political efforts and heroic oratorical performances—the following year. Yet impeachment did not mean conviction, a decision reserved to the House of Lords, where Hastings's political connections (and, in some instances, the thinness of Burke's evidence) made acquittal a foregone conclusion. Burke was positive, however, that vital principles were at stake, and while defeat was inevitable, he grappled with a lost cause until the Lords found Hastings innocent in 1795.

Achievement and Agony

Like many lives, Burke's was a mixture of fulfillment and frustration. From distinctly modest origins, and with handicaps he did not himself impose, he rose to a position of eminence in British public life. By dint of sheer ability, he was assured of an audience whenever he wished to speak. He commanded respect, if not agreement, in the most impressive intellectual circles. In the second half of the eighteenth century, there was not a British mind whose work is worth remembering with which Burke was not in close touch, often personally. He had achieved a certain standing, and he had as well—no small thing when primogeniture was still one of the first rules of society—a son to whom he hoped to pass it on.

On the other hand, he had never exercised power, and it was clear by the mid-1780s that he never would. He had the ear of the wealthy, but they also held his notes: he was in debt to the Rockingham family for much of his later life, and it took a controversial government pension toward the end to resolve the financial unpleasantness which had persistently nagged him. His gifts were impressive, including one for political failure. It was rare when he found himself, or his associates, carrying the day. Burke was best known, by the time he reached sixty, for his stands on America, India, and Ireland; he had lost them all.

Events gave him one last chance to play the role of conscience for the constitution, and he used the opportunity to obtain immortality. The French revolution of 1789, as any more than casual student of Burke's career could then have seen, flaunted every political and indeed moral article of Burke's creed. His volcanic response, the *Reflections on the Revolution in France* (1790), is the most impressive piece of political writing in English history, arguably among the greatest examples of English prose ever. It both summed up his political philosophy to date and incorporated some largely unstated tenets. It sparked a public debate which shattered his own party and made of Burke a figure of whom no moderate judgment was possible. One was either with Burke or against him, a situation he encouraged with such later writings as *An Appeal from the New to the Old Whigs* (1791), *A Letter to a Member of the French National Assembly* (1791), and the *Letters on a Regicide Peace* (1796–97).

Still he despaired. Revolutionary France went from political extremism to military success, and although England joined the European coalition against the French in 1793, Burke feared for the will of the allies and worried that the war effort would stop short of completely extirpating revolution on the Continent and preventing its spread across the channel. He retired from Parliament in 1794, at the age of sixty-five, but within months, personal tragedy bore in upon him. In February 1794, his brother Richard died, and in July of the same year, so too did Burke's son, Richard.

It is scarcely exaggeration to say that Burke worshiped his son, and it seems unlikely that either of them experienced a closer emotional bond in their lives. Predictably, perhaps, the famous father was convinced that the star of his heir would outshine his own— so convinced that. he was blind to Richard's rather meager talents and to the fact that such accomplishments as the young man could point to stemmed largely from an accident of birth. During the 1790s, Richard helped his father with his political writings and undertook a complex mission of intrigue to the French émigrés in Germany and later another political journey to Ireland. From the handful of surviving letters, however, there is little impressive about the young man's imagination, powers of observation, or ability to express himself—anything, for that matter, beyond his aggressive devotion to his father.

For a man of such intelligence, Burke had gargantuan powers of self-delusion, especially about his family. His artistry in dogged commitment to the hopeless cause matched Pope's with the heroic couplet. He had convinced his son and himself that Richard would follow him in a parliamentary career more brilliant than his own. As it happened, Richard has found his way into the pages of history only by causing his father inconsolable grief. Burke had expected that all the disappointment of his life, felt so keenly toward its end, could be redeemed by his son's career. Instead, he was left to live, and to die, with greater pain still.

There was even more to come. The year 1795 brought the inevitable acquittal of Hastings in the House of Lords, and 1796 public criticism of the government pension granted Burke which allowed him to resolve his chronically ruinous finances. It was, at least, an occasion which allowed Burke to leave a little of that pain behind. He answered his detractors—with appropriate irony, the principal one was a great Whig nobleman, the Duke of Bedford— with a furious polemic, *A Letter to a Noble Lord* (1796), the pure anger of which has yet to be surpassed in English political writing.

Burke could not know that successive generations would commemorate him as a towering figure in English politics and intellectual life; the bitterness of his enemies was more immediate. When he died in 1797, it was after leaving instructions that he be buried in a secret and anonymous grave, lest his remains be desecrated. To this date, they have not been located.

Chapter Two

Humanism and the Moral Voice

Burke was a politician. He expressed his political views, however, with such force and grace that he must also be taken seriously as a writer, and not simply a political writer. Both quantitatively and qualitatively, his political works were his most important, but they issued from a mind shaped in grappling with a variety of other questions. Some of the configurations of that mind deserve special attention just as Burke the writer merits special consideration.

The Political Man of Letters

Burke is anthologized in countless collections of political philosophy, yet to locate his work in the tradition of systematic thought which includes Hobbes, Locke, and Mill (to name only Englishmen) surely misleads. His writings tended to deal with the occasional, the crisis of the moment; his mind was empirical and tended to avoid abstraction. He was not prone to define the concept of justice, but rather to seek some version of it for (say) the Irish Catholics in the here and now. System interested him less than convenience. Moreover, it is difficult to read him and feel in the presence of an exploratory intelligence, examining possibilities and evaluation options in a search for truth. Burke always seemed to know the answer before the question had been asked. He did not probe, he announced, and he was not embarrassed to say that the positions he announced were often received opinions. We read Burke today not so much because he formulated startlingly novel ideas, but because he argued old ideas in original and effective ways.

Burke was not so much a philosopher as a philosophical polemicist, a talented controversialist attempting to persuade his audience. (One only has to compare his one foray into something like formal philosophy, the *Philosophical Enquiry,* with almost everything else

11

he wrote, to appreciate the point.) The word has fallen into ill
repute or we would call Burke a propagandist—one who practiced
the art of generating conviction. Or perhaps we can take one of his
own terms somewhat out of context and think of Burke as a "Political
Man of Letters."[1]

The man of letters is a rare species, having been thinned drastically
by the parcelizing effects of the industrial revolution and its insistence upon specialization and the division of labor. Adam Smith's
pin factory nearly spelled the end of men like Burke, whom Smith
admired, and also of Smith himself, who wrote on psychology as
well as political economy. In time, one would need professional
credentials to write, or at least to write credibly, on politics, aesthetics, history, religion, drama, political economy—all subjects of
Burke's. In the eighteenth century, however, classical education
rendered such diversification common.

Education was then, of course, extended only to the elite—the
well born, and those sufficiently well-to-do to afford schooling. Yet
the whole point of education was in a curious sense democratic: to
create a vocabulary and a set of referents which put educated men
on an equal intellectual footing. The curriculum was, by modern
standards, limited; it rarely encompassed more than classical lan-
guages, literature, history, philosophy, and theology. This comparative narrowness, however, actually promoted breadth of
knowledge. Students might prefer one subject to another, but they
were not allowed to "specialize." What they were taught, they were
expected to know; it was all important.

It was important for its substance. Cicero and Milton had intrinsic
merit. There were certain things an educated man was expected to
know for their own sake. But the eighteenth-century curriculum
was also important for the mental discipline it encouraged. Young
men were expected to learn Latin not because it was difficult to
obtain reliable translations of ancient texts but because the exercise
was deemed salutary. Again, the idea was to produce intellectual
generalists by constantly building certain mental skills—memory,
logic, analysis—which could be applied to any subject. If a man
could read knowledgeably on a variety of subjects, what was to stop
him from writing on a variety of subjects?

Even for his time, the scope of Burke's interest and accomplishment was prodigious. His curiosity was almost Faustian, his grasp
legendary. He consorted regularly with the best minds of his age

and more than held his own. Poets, painters, actors, philosophers, historians, playwrights—astoundingly, for a man with a full political career, Burke knew virtually all of them who counted for anything. A study of his literary friendships reads like a companion to eighteenth-century English literature.[2] It is hard to think of another contemporary in closer touch with so many dimensions of cultural life.

It was not merely breadth, however, which characterized the man of letters. He was expected to write wisely, but also well. In the eighteenth century, clarity was taken for granted and eloquence expected. The small but demanding reading audience appreciated and encouraged a subtle allusion, a resonant metaphor, a delicately balanced periodic sentence, an extensively sustained analogy. A case can be made that the age bracketed by Swift and Burke, and which included among others Johnson, Hume, Gibbon, Addison, and Boswell, produced the richest of all English prose.

Yet the man of letters was not satisfied to serve aesthetic ends only. His work was serious and like the classical literature that educated him, his writing was highly charged with moral purpose. The history, the literature, and the philosophy of antiquity which figured so predominantly in a classical education were highly didactic. Livy's account of the Roman Republic was not meant to be a compendium of reliable facts, but a series of civic lessons broadly applicable to other times. A tragedy by Sophocles not only contained moral advice, but was as well a formal statement about order, balance, restraint.

It was important to amuse eighteenth-century readers, but it was not enough. Most writers took literature as a vehicle for strenuous moral argument, and therefore a medium of the highest seriousness. Precisely because they were trained as generalists, men of letters were able to locate moral significance in a variety of circumstances, an act which comes close to defining their principal function.

Early Works

We can see Burke, the young man of letters, in two books with which he attempted to launch his literary career in 1756. Both were remarkably mature in conception and execution, and both, as it turned out, were touched with intellectual and stylistic trademarks which his writings would carry throughout his life.

Decades later, Burke asked, "Who now reads Bolingbroke? Who ever read him through?" One answer to these disdainful questions is, Burke himself, probably not long after the 1754 edition of Bolingbroke's works appeared (some three years after their author's death). Henry St. John, Viscount Bolingbroke, had been a politician and an essayist on a wide range of subjects; Burke, however, chose to concentrate on the implications of his religious views. Bolingbroke was a deist, which meant that he discarded revelation and the many bewildering mysteries of the Christian faith for an approach to religion through human reason. Those religious beliefs which would survive rational scrutiny would be few in number yet entirely adequate to God's purposes; they would be simple, direct, comprehensible, personal, in short "natural"—rooted neither in tradition nor in the dictates of institutionalized churches.

These were views with which Burke had scant sympathy. Feelings, and not reason, were more trustworthy guides in religion. In some jottings from the early 1750s, he wrote approvingly of those persons who "naturally measure their Duties to the Divinity by their own wants and their feelings, and not by abstract Speculations. In the one they cannot be deceived, in the other they may."[3] Yet he chose to attack Bolingbroke's deism indirectly by following what he took to be its consequences for political philosophy.

As it happened, the whole essay nearly misfired, for Burke cast it in the form of a satire. Its full title was *A Vindication of Natural Society, or, A View of the Miseries and Evils Arising to Mankind from Every Species of Artificial Society, in a Letter to Lord **** by a Late Noble Writer.* It appeared without Burke's name, and so the only "voice" one hears is that of the narrator or "Late Noble Writer," Bolingbroke. Moreover, Burke captured certain features of that voice with great deftness—the ironic tone, the insincere self-effacement, the pretentious but often suspect scholarship, the florid rhetoric followed by disclaimers such as "I have purposely avoided a parade of eloquence on this occasion." The difficulty was that Burke's strategy was one of indirection. He wished to demonstrate that "logical" argument from false premises could lead to conclusions that were wholly plausible yet at bottom unacceptable. As he explained in a preface to the second edition in 1757: "The design was to show that, without the exertion of any considerable forces, the same engines which were employed for the destruction of religion, might be employed with equal success for the subversion of government; and that specious arguments might be used against those things which they, who doubt of everything else, will never permit to be questioned."[4] In the accomplishment of his design, however, Burke made his narrator's case with enough force that certain reviewers took the *Vindication* for advocacy rather than satire.

On the first page, Burke had his narrator begin a discussion of politics just where a deist would begin a discussion of religion—by calling for a frank and critical examination of all questions and insisting upon the ability of human reason to conduct it. Then followed a familiar sketch of "natural society," that is, the prepolitical state of nature in which society consisted only of the individual family. In opposition to it, he described "political" or "artificial society," in which the individual families associated in a body politic bound together by laws.

He then proceeded to the alleged defects of artificial society. Its history in all times and places had been characterized first of all by warfare between the several societies (or states). Burke's narrator launched into a colorful survey of war's ravages ("I need not enlarge on those torrents of silent and inglorious blood which have glutted the thirsty sands of Afric, or discolored the polar snow . . ."[5]) and asserted, with a flourish of arithmetical legerdemain, that they had claimed perhaps seventy times the number of lives which then inhabited the earth. Carnage on such an epic scale would be impossible in natural society, he insisted, because one could not unite enough men behind a single purpose to organize much more than a brawl. In political society, however, institutions such as armies had maximized both the possibility and the destructiveness of war, and the very existence of numerous states encouraged rivalries and jealousies.

If artificial society could not avoid costly external conflict, neither could it escape internal distress. Burke's narrator argued that no form of government can foster liberty. Despotism was the tyranny of one man, aristocracy the tyranny of a few, democracy the tyranny of many (most of whom were unfit to rule in the first place). Nor was a "mixed government"—combining elements of each—any solution. Compromise among monarch, nobility, and populace was rare and difficult to attain. The separate groups tended to form parties, whose "spirit of ambition, of self-interest, of oppression and treachery . . . entirely reverses all the principles which a benevolent nature has erected within us. . . ."[6]

It was no consolation that political society, of whatever form, might claim to operate under a rule of law. For the law was an arcane body of technical propositions, its interpretation left to an elite guild. With great glee, and no doubt recalling his own unhappy experiences at the Middle Temple, Burke thundered at the inability of lawyers to agree upon interpretations, the consequent multiplication of laws which only compounded the confusion, the numerous instances where technicalities aborted justice, the ridiculous delay in civil cases which often immobilized property, and the untoward haste which was common in capital crimes ("that great question in which no delay ought to be counted tedious . . .")[7].

Finally, Burke's narrator laid at the door of artificial society the unequal distribution of property which vested wealth in the hands of a few and condemned so many to cruel and unrewarding labor. The poor, he insisted, were in a condition scarcely distinguishable from slavery: "nine parts in ten of the whole race of mankind drudge through life."[8] The rich were either mere pleasure seekers, in the end enervated by luxury, or politically ambitious, insatiable lusters after a power which "gradually extirpates from the mind every humane and gentle virtue."[9] If it were to be argued that this inequality was vital to bring about "the arts which cultivate life," then the narrator would ask how those arts in their turn became necessary. The answer, he expected, would be that civil society could not exist without them—a patently circular mode of reasoning.

None of these evils would be present, or even possible, in natural society. Without nations, there could be no wars. Without governments of any sort, there could be no tyranny. Without laws, there could be no institutionalized injustice, no secular priesthood to puzzle out the Delphic utterances of the statutes. Where "a man's acquisitions are in proportion to his labors," there would be no radical discrepancies in the distribution of property. In natural society, "Life is simple, and therefore it is happy." Natural society alone offered "perfect liberty."[10]

It was not merely the conclusions of this argument that Burke wished to discredit. His departure from the narrator's position came at the very outset, with that proclamation of confidence in human reason. Since Burke really did believe that there were things one should "never permit to be questioned," he was convinced that "a mind which has no restraint from a sense of its own weakness, of its subordinate rank in the creation, and of the extreme danger of letting the imagination loose upon some subjects, may very plausibly attack everything the most excellent and venerable. . . ."[11] Even before publishing the *Vindication,* Burke had privately concluded that to depart from long-established human ways was to ignore human limitations: "A man who considers his nature rightly will be diffident of any reasonings that carry him out of the ordinary roads of life. . . . There is some general principle operating to produce Customs, that is a more sure guide than our Theories."[12]

"Bolingbroke," at least in Burke's hands, became a monger of abstractions, including that snare and delusion "perfect liberty." The whole underlying argument of the *Vindication* was directed squarely at the narrator's opening declaration that "to know whether any proposition be true or false, it is a preposterous method to examine it by its apparent consequences."[13] For Burke, it was exactly the consequences of any proposition that demanded the first consideration. What, he was asking between the lines, would transpire if we removed government and law from the face of the earth? What would it be like if we obliterated social distinctions? Though war had its tragic and wasteful side, can we really imagine a world without nations? Moreover, how do we go about renouncing the institutions of "artificial" society? Even if it were desirable, how would one undo the work of countless generations?

Burke was also at pains to show that the reverse face of this pernicious politics was clearly stamped "deism." He had his "Bolingbroke" maintain: "Civil government borrows a strength from ecclesiastical; and artificial laws receive a sanction from artificial revelations. The ideas of religion and government are closely connected; and whilst we receive government as a thing necessary, or even useful to our well-being, we shall in spite of us draw in, as a necessary, though undesirable consequence, an artificial religion of some kind or another."[14] But then of course the contrary was true as well: a deist could not reconcile his position with an acceptance of "artificial" society. Accept political institutions, and you are perforce wedded to "artificial" religion. The religious side of Burke's argument was as important as the political, or rather was the basis of it. For deism, he insisted, led directly to a politics of thinking the unthinkable.

Burke's views on human nature, government, and society had not entirely matured by 1756, but their shape was emerging. He would circumscribe the domain of human reason and exempt certain fun-

damental institutions and practices from analysis. He respected the
heritage of the past, including traditionally established religion.
Political society was ineradicable, unequal distribution of property
most likely unavoidable. He was, in sum, making a commitment
to the broad contours of things as they were and suggesting that
any proposal for change had to be evaluted in terms of its impact
upon those contours, not its logical consistency or abstract appeal.

There was an empiricist strain to the *Vindication*. Burke wanted
to know what the world, the real world around us, would look like
if it were refashioned according to some "rational" theory. The same
disposition reappeared in a second book he published in 1756, *A
Philosophical Enquiry into the Origin of Our Ideas of the Sublime and
Beautiful*. It was a much longer work than the *Vindication*—longer
by more than three times when Burke revised and expanded it for
a second edition the next year—and one upon which he had apparently been working since his days at Trinity.[15]

The *Enquiry* was a wide-ranging treatise which touched on physiology, psychology, philosophy, and aesthetics, and both cited and
took issue with authorities ancient and modern. What gave it unity
was Burke's thoroughgoing sensationist orientation. Human aesthetic responses, including even taste itself, he argued, began with
the senses; the mind only intervened to help sort out sensory impres-
sions. This was of course to dispute the classical views that an
intellectual regard for proportion or an appreciation of moral qualities inhering in a work of art were at the core of aesthetic response.
The distinction between the beautiful and the sublime rested upon
a more familiar and at bottom physiological one—that between
pleasure and pain. In large part, his thesis turned on the contention
that while human beings sought pleasure, they even more ardently
sought to avoid pain: "Without all doubt, the torments which we
may be made to suffer are much greater in their effect on the body
and mind, than any pleasures which the most learned voluptuary
could suggest, or than the liveliest imagination, and the most sound
and exquisitely sensible body, could enjoy."[16] One would be hard
put, thought Burke, to find a man who would accept "a life of the
most perfect satisfaction" if he knew in advance that at its end
waited a few hours on the rack.

It was precisely for these reasons that the sublime generated
stronger reactions, for it had its source in terror, in the fear of danger
or pain or death. The beautiful, on the other hand, while productive

of pleasure, led to far less affecting emotions. With beauty, one was in the company of the small, the delicate, the graceful—none of which could threaten or astonish. With the sublime, one confronted that which was vast, incomprehensible, and above all superior in power—characteristics which were, Burke reminded us, also those of the Deity.

The *Enquiry* gives us yet another perspective on the breadth of Burke's early interests. It provides further indication of his notions of human beings as creatures with a vast reservoir of passions. It reminds us that he was a man of strong religious feelings, yet harbored a distinctly empirical bent in philosophical matters. But its significance is greater for the history of aesthetics than for the study of Burke's intellectual development. The book brought him a European reputation; it helped crystallize certain of Diderot's ideas and had its influence upon men like Lessing and Kant as well.[17] Its version of the sublime anticipated certain Romantic preoccupations with the Gothic. But while it was consistent with much of his later thought, it did not suggest the direction which that thought might take.

A short history of England, which Burke was unable to carry beyond the Magna Carta, is somewhat more instructive. Unpublished in his lifetime, it appears in his *Works* under the title *An Essay Toward an Abridgement of the English History* and runs to around 90,000 words. It reveals Burke as a serious and even skilled historian, generally conscious of possible shortcomings or biases in his sources, concerned to present balanced judgments, and accomplished in the presentation of narrative detail. Not that the work is "pure narrative." The influence of Montesquieu, to whom he refers as "The greatest genius which has enlightened this age," was apparent from the outset, where Burke took up the relationship of climate to social and cultural behavior. There were also several lengthy discussions of custom, of religion, and of law.

For the most part, however, Burke wrote a history of statecraft and warfare from the Roman conquest until the early thirteenth century, and his central characters were kings and great lords—which is simply to say that his approach was orthodox for the time. He assigned praise and blame without inhibition, but equally without pettiness or *parti pris*. The men who populate his pages were meant to be exemplary of good or bad statesmanship. His treatment of the Saxon king Alfred was typical: ". . . whatever dark spots of

human frailty may have adhered to such a character, they are entirely
hid in the splendor of his many shining qualities and grand virtues,
that throw a glory over the obscure period in which he lived, and
which is for no other reason worthy of our knowledge."[18] Similarly,
Burke could think of "nothing more memorable in history than the
actions, fortunes, and character" of William the Conqueror, "whether
we consider the grandeur of the plans he formed, the courage and
wisdom with which they were executed, or the splendor of that
success which, adorning his youth, continued without the smallest
reverse to support his age, even to the last moments of his life."[19]

Burke was also sensitive to the course of constitutional development. Thus, while he had much praise for the character of Thomas
à Becket and deplored the manner of his death, he could only
conclude that Becket's conception of church power was "subversive
of all good government."[20] While largely favorable to the barons
who imposed the Magna Carta on King John, still Burke was disturbed that they had gone too far and "scarcely left a shadow of
regal power."[21]

In general, Burke awarded his approval to behavior (even when
violent) which promoted orderly government, decisions which secured old liberties or cautiously created new ones, policies which
maintained the balance of traditional authorities and institutions or
rearranged the balance in a more workable fashion, practices which
reaffirmed the role of religion but kept zealous clerics from aggran-
dizing the government at the profit of the Church. It was a utilitarian
sanction, not the only sort he ever employed, but one as central to
the *Abridgement* as to the *Vindication*.

The *Vindication* and the *Abridgement* announce the affinity for
politics which would soon dominate Burke's writings. Before examining that work, however, it is important to consider some of
the pervasive intellectual preferences and mental habits which run
through most of what he wrote.

The Propensities of Humanism

Burke assumed that historical consciousness was a reflex of the
educated mind: ". . . there are a few statesmen so very clumsy and
awkward in their business, as to fall into the identical snare which
has proved fatal to their predecessors."[22] Much of the satire of the
Vindication lay in the pretentious parade of false history and in the

implied conclusion that no examination of the past could possibly support the idea of a "natural" society.

History was a story to be studied for its useful lessons, but as a collection of past human decisions and actions it was also an agent. History tested courses of behavior. It created present circumstances and in the process it eliminated certain options. It created social conditions which could no more be overlooked than the law of gravity. That which was inborn in human beings, such as reason, was feeble and trifling—only as old as the individual—compared to that which had been shaped and handed down by the generations.[23] It was here that Burke's intellectual habits and his intellectual preferences joined.

Burke's use of history, and his preoccupations in general, were the more concrete for being insistently human. He would have been appalled by a later age's taste for a bloodless past in which "forces" and "factors" operated. History was human decision, politics was calculation based upon human nature, literature was an analysis of the human moral condition. Burke's writings have a pulse-beat in them because he was interested in character, personality, and foible, because he dealt with "principle" and "right" in recognizable human terms.

Typically, Burke personalized great public questions, sometimes in rather shadowy generalizations ("the Americans," "the nobility of France"), but more often in vivid human detail. The most famous instance was his outburst in the midst of the *Reflections* on the humiliation of Marie Antoinette, which stood for the degradation of all persons of rank.[24] But there were numerous other examples, from General Conway in the "Speech on American Taxation" to the unfortunate Hafiz Rhamet in the speech on Fox's East India Bill:

. . . the most eminent of their chiefs, one of the bravest men of his time, and as famous throughout the East for the elegance of his literature and the spirit of his poetical compositions . . . as for his courage, was invaded with an army of an hundred thousand men, and an English brigade. This man, at the head of inferior forces, was slain valiantly fighting for his country. His head was cut off, and delivered for money to a barbarian. His wife and children, persons of that rank, were seen begging an handful of rice through the English camp. The whole nation, with inconsiderable exceptions, was slaughtered or banished.[25]

Burke also humanized and personalized his work with the frequent
introduction of himself. It was more than a matter of the "I" common to oratory. Burke customarily reached out to his reader with
a voice which was unique and warmed by personal anecdote. His
"I" had weight and substance because he often accompanied it with
a second-person singular, a "you" to whom he addressed questions,
paid compliments, and offered admonitions. The humanistic tenor
of Burke's writing lies in the fact that it was addressed to people
before posterity.

Perhaps most important, people were Burke's subject. For him,
questions of state were generally, upon close examination, questions
of human nature. In a famous passage, he connected the two explicitly: ". . . He who gave our nature to be perfected by our virtue
willed also the necessary means of its perfection: He willed, therefore, the state. . . ."[26] But his conviction that political—and historical, and aesthetic, and religious, and virtually all—issues were
only so many approaches to human nature was everywhere apparent
in his work.

It was not an unorthodox position in a century whose epigraph
could easily read: "The proper study of mankind is man." Burke
has properly been located toward the end of an ethical tradition
which wholly lived up to Pope's injunction, and did so from a
distinct point of view.[27] An honest investigation of the human past,
Burke and his forebears in this tradition were convinced, led to
certain unavoidable and unflattering conclusions about human nature.

The *philosophes* did not discover the idea of progress, but many
of them did their share to promote the notion that human reason
was capable of creating a better—even vastly better—world. While
Burke would have agreed that material progress was everywhere
obvious, he would have drawn the line at moral progress. Human
life may have been better in the eighteenth century than in the
eighth, but it was questionable that human beings were. Human
passions, human inclinations, human will were as refractory and
dangerous as ever, fully as suspicious as a later writer found them:

. . . men are not gentle creatures who want to be loved, and who at the
most can defend themselves if they are attacked; they are, on the contrary,
creatures among whose instinctual endowments is to be reckoned a powerful share of aggressiveness. As a result, their neighbour is for them not
only a potential helper or sexual object, but also someone who tempts

them to satisfy their aggressiveness on him, to exploit his capacity for work without compensation, to use him sexually without his consent, to seize his possessions, to humiliate him, to cause him pain, to torture and to kill him. *Homo homini lupus.* Who, in the face of all his experience of life and of history, will have the courage to dispute this assertion?[28]

Like Freud, Burke came to exactly this conclusion by a secular path—an awareness of the human past—but he traveled a parallel religious route as well. Christianity taught the irreducible nugget of human perversity, original sin. God's most righteous servant was still flawed. As a Christian, and as a man preoccupied with human behavior, Burke was led to a skeptical and ultimately tragic appraisal of the human condition.

It was important that humans accept this condition, not as an unfortunate accident but as part of the divine will: there was, after all, an "Author of our nature." It was the work of the man of letters to persuade toward that acceptance, to adjust human behavior to human nature. It was in this sense, once more, that literature served a principally moral function.

For Burke, then, the most persistent cause of discord in human affairs was the failure to recognize and accept the flaws of human nature, the tendency to suppose that humans were more reasonable than they could be, less the captives of their passions, unlikely to do harm when they wished to do good. At times, he tried to meet this failing with sweet reason. The two great American speeches were models of good sense and good humor. *Thoughts on the Cause of the Present Discontents* was, for the most part, a sober and restrained venture in a subject—political factionalism and constitutional subversion—which had invited more inflammatory rhetoric. Yet these and a few lesser cases are exceptions. Burke was not a patient man. One of the reasons why he was the subject of so much obliquy and public bitterness was that he dealt out so much in his turn. If his writing has a characteristic tone, it is anger, sometimes expressed in mockery and ridicule, just as often in undiluted rage.

It is always possible that the most fruitful approach to Burke's anger is psychoanalytical, although recent efforts have done little to inspire confidence.[29] In any case, it is clear that Burke could be hurt by disappointments in his career, personal insults, and what a later age would call status anxieties, and that he transformed his pain into fury. The most celebrated example is *A Letter to a Noble*

Lord, which answered questions raised by the Duke of Bedford about the appropriateness of the government pension being offered Burke as he ended his political career. He began by insisting, "I at least have nothing to complain of," whereupon he proceeded to butcher the duke in some of the grandest immoderate prose known to man. He reminded that, just as his own pension comes from the government, so did most of the wealth of Bedford's house:

The grants to the House of Russell were so enormous as not only to outrage economy, but even to stagger credibility. The Duke of Bedford is the leviathan among all the creatures of the crown. He tumbles about his unwieldy bulk, he plays and frolics in the ocean of the royal bounty. Huge as he is, and whilst "he lies floating many a rood," he is still a creature. His ribs, his fins, his whalebone, his blubber, the very spiracles through which he spouts a torrent of brine against his origin, and covers me all over with the spray, everything of him and about him is from the throne. Is it for *him* to question the dispensation of the royal favor?[30]

Yet it was not simply invective aroused by insult which defined Burke's anger. In a time often thought to be symbolized by elaborate ritual and extravagant courtesy, Burke raged at human arrogance, shortsightedness, and stupidity.

Even casual students of Burke are familiar with the colossal fury of his later years, marked as they were with political defeat, personal tragedy, and the apocalyptic threat of the French Revolution. Yet his writing had often before been mottled with anger; human flaws and human obduracy had frequently ignited him. In 1781, for example, when it appeared that the crown condoned the confiscation of certain British subjects' private property in the West Indies, Burke was not satisfied to criticize. Instead, he began defining the terms under which a monarch "must give up his royalty and his government. . . ."[31] In a speech on a minor bill in the same year, he quickly escalated from a discussion of legislative details to a fantasy of civil war:

I have incurred the odium of gentlemen in this House for not paying sufficient regard to men of ample property. When, indeed, the smallest rights of the poorest people in the kingdom are in question, I would set my face against any act of pride and power countenanced by the highest that are in it; and if it should come to the last extremity, and to a contest of blood,—God forbid! God forbid!—my part is taken: I would take my fate with the poor and low and feeble. But if these people came to turn their liberty into a cloak for maliciousness, and to seek a privilege of exemption, not from power, but from the rules of morality and virtuous discipline, then I would join my hand to make them feel the force which a few united in a good cause have over a multitude of the profligate and ferocious.[32]

Sarcasm, the blunter cousin of satire, was one of Burke's habitual resorts. The *Reflections* is perhaps unique among the classics of Western thought for its consistently derisive tone, its impatience with delicate irony when nastiness could get the job done. Burke wrote of obscure parish priests elected to the Estates-General "who had never seen the state so much as in a picture. . . ."[33] He dismissed an antagonist with "Rousseau, in one of his lucid intervals . . ." and the idea of democracy in a famous gibe: "It is said that twenty-four millions ought to prevail over two hundred thousand. True; if the constitution of a kingdom be a problem of arithmetic. This sort of discourse does well enough with the lamp-post for its second: to men who *may* reason calmly it is ridiculous."[34]

Elements of Style

"I find a preacher of the gospel prophaning the beautiful and prophetic ejaculation, commonly called '*nunc dimittis,*' made on the first presentation of our Saviour in the Temple, and applying it, with an inhuman and unnatural rapture, to the most horrid, atrocious, and afflicting spectacle that perhaps ever was exhibited to the pity and indignation of mankind." It is difficult to imagine that anyone other than Burke could have written this sentence, plucked more or less at random from the *Reflections,* so clearly is his stamp upon it.

To begin with, the sentence is long, and Burke liked long sentences, liked the rhythms they permitted him and the opportunities they afforded for protracted crescendos building to thunderous climaxes. It is not, however, merely a question of prose metrics. In the sentence above, there is no padding for the sake of euphonics. It is impossible to remove any of the words, phrases, or clauses without weakening the impact. Long sentences, when skillfully executed, can have a powerful cumulative impact, and Burke was seeking power—the power to convince. In this instance, we begin with the arresting vision of a man who is nominally a spokesman for God "prophaning" a term with sacred associations. The preacher goes farther, however, inhumanly and unnaturally, and before we can catch our breath we learn that he has done perhaps the worst thing in the history of the world. It is not easy to resist the movement of that long sentence as it builds to its final condemnation, and it is obvious that short, compact, easily digestible sentences would not have done.

Burke also freely employed virtually every known rhetorical device, a fact to which new and perhaps unsuspecting readers should be alert. He was frequently alliterative ("prophaning . . . prophetic") and hyperbolic ("the most horrid . . ."). He would alternate his long, rolling sentences with extremely brief ones. He was not afraid of violent language or exotic metaphors, of direct appeals to sentiment or rough, sarcastic humor. He adored launching barrages of rhetorical questions. He could polish a transition to a high sheen or work one abruptly to jolt a reader's responses. His vocabulary was enormous and he gave the impression that he wanted to use it all in everything he wrote. In all this, he was not simply out for a good time, writing for catharsis, showing off. Burke's ends were political: he sought to persuade. He was a supremely manipulative writer.

Clearly, the format of Burke's writings once he had taken up a parliamentary career owed much to that of the speech. He used direct address to establish intimate contact with his audience. He moved easily from tone to tone—informative and descriptive, conversational and confiding, hortatory and declamatory. Since the epistolary form provided many of the same advantages, he employed it often.

In any event, there was nothing especially novel or characteristic about his organization. He might open abruptly or move leisurely to his point, finish with an epic crash or wind down in a long conclusion. His transitions and joinings might be subtle and artful, as in the *Reflections,* a work he spent months in polishing, or harsh and sudden, as in the several letters on a regicide peace. His true genius was not so much in architecture, the total plan of a piece, as in interior design—the sentence, the paragraph, the passage.

Burke was an almost magically concise writer, and while his Latinate sentences may baffle the modern reader accustomed to telegrammatic prose, they carried an uncommon amount of information, attitude, persuasive ammunition, and sensitivity to various audiences. Let the following two paragraphs from *Thoughts on the Cause of the Present Discontents* serve as a case for close reading:

> It is true, that the peers have a great influence in the kingdom, and in every part of the public concerns. While they are men of property, it is impossible to prevent it, except by such means as must prevent all property from its natural operation: an event not easily to be compassed, while property is power; nor by any means to be wished, while the least notion exists of the method by which the spirit of liberty acts, and of the means by which it is preserved. If any particular peers, by their uniform, upright, constitutional conduct, by their public and their private virtues, have acquired an influence in the country; the people, on whose favor that influence depends, and from whom it arose, will never be duped into an opinion, that such greatness in a peer is the despotism of an aristocracy, when they know and feel it to be the effect and pledge of their own importance.
>
> I am no friend to aristocracy, in the sense at least in which that word is usually understood. If it were not a bad habit to moot cases on the supposed ruin of the constitution, I should be free to declare, that if it must perish, I would rather by far see it resolved into any other form, than lost in that austere and insolent domination. But, whatever my dislikes may be, my fears are not upon that quarter. The question, on the influence of a court, and of a peerage, is not, which of the two dangers is the more eligible, but which is the more imminent. He is but a poor observer, who has not seen, that the generality of peers, far from supporting themselves in a state of independent greatness, are but too apt to fall into an oblivion of their proper dignity, and to run headlong into an abject servitude. Would to God it were true, that the fault of our peers were too much spirit. . . .[35]

Burke's task here was no simple one. He wanted to defend the aristocracy against democratic criticism while at the same time prodding the peerage into more aggressive political action. He had to speak for the aristocracy without appearing to be their paid mouthpiece. He wished to find a credible independent voice while promoting a powerful traditional establishment.

It is a nimble pasage, one in which Burke began by stating the obvious and then immediately discovered that it was both inevitable and richly to be desired. The peerage was, at bottom, great property, the ascendancy of which was both "impossible to prevent" and—to come to much the same conclusion with a word charged with very different evocative power—"natural." Yet the unavoidable and the natural also turned out to be wholly salutary. Here Burke could mention property and liberty in the same breath, although without elaboration, and be confident that he had plucked a responsive string in many of his readers—for whom it was orthodoxy that private property offered independence, and therefore freedom from external control, and that great concentrations of property were vital for the protection of lesser amounts. By avoiding an argumentative tone— he was much closer to "It goes without saying"—Burke glided quickly through what was in fact a highly arguable point, nailing down a premise in the guise of an eternal verity.

The next sentence—"If any particular peers . . ."—is especially deft. In reasonably few words, Burke succeeded in suggesting that any aristocratic influence stemmed only from the most laudable civic behavior, then suddenly ascribing that influence neither to civic virtue nor to inherited wealth but rather the "favor" of the commons, whom he then complimented and invited to compliment themselves for their perspicacity in recognizing that aristocratic influence only underscored the importance of the commons. In one paragraph, devoid of florid language—although the verb "duped" performed a crucial function in the final sentence—Burke justified a political and social system on the grounds that it was inevitable, in the nature of things, preferable, the result of noble deeds, and—as everyone knew—in the best interests of all.

In the second paragraph, Burke cemented this justification with a startling change of tactics. Read the opening sentence and see which clause is liable to stick in the mind. Having offered a clever and subtle defense of aristocracy, Burke then presented a surprising set of *bona fides:* "I am no friend to aristocracy. . . ." The subsequent reference to "austere and insolent domination" is in fact directed more at a form of government than at a social order, and as such would hardly stand as a repudiation of what had gone before, however differently it read. Burke then appeared neatly to resolve principles and practicality by giving the distinct impression of swallowing his personal inclinations for the public good. Then to the attack: it was the influence of the court, and not the peerage, which was "imminent." The obvious truth with which the passage began— "It is true, that the peers have a great influence in the kingdom, and in every part of the public concerns"—has been replaced by an image of the aristocracy as dispirited layabouts, men for whom "abject servitude" was more congenial than "independent greatness."

Finally, Burke concluded the movement from the lofty eminence of "great influence" at the outset to "abject servitude" at the end, a movement of tragic decline tagged with a prayerful flutter of hope: "Would to God it were true, that the fault of our peers were too much spirit."

The paragraphs have an absorbing rhythm, a phrasing which asks to be read aloud, and there is an arresting change of pace achieved by the long periodic sentence which concludes the first paragraph and the pungent, faintly combative clause which opens the second. Yet it would be mistaken to take this display of verbal agility for mere manipulation. Burke genuinely believed that the best social arrangements were multiply justifiable. A thing which was necessary was in most instances also good, preferable, and natural. Moreover, he was convinced that his political role entailed not merely the forceful statement of his (largely aristocratic) party's policy but also the exercise of persuasion within the party. He commonly tried to nudge his social betters in this direction or that, as his correspondence demonstrates. The important lesson is that Burke could combine political skill with conviction and both of them with an exceptional power to pack words and meanings densely. He must, in most cases, be read with this sort of care and attention.

Burke's masterful use of imagery has been the subject of analysis elsewhere.[36] But while one cannot help but be struck by his figurative conceits, it is also interesting to note how little he indulged himself in them. Burke was a direct writer, and his figures were doubtless the more effective for his having employed them sparingly. The rich texture of his prose results not from extended images but once again from the concise use of metaphorical nouns, verbs, and adjectives.

In a published letter of 1777, Burke wrote that liberty "is not only a private blessing of the first order, but the vital spring and energy of the state itself, which has just so much life and vigor as there is liberty in it."[37] The ability of this sentence to summon an affirmative response in us lies in the fact that we do *not* pause to quibble that, strictly speaking, a state cannot have a "spring" or "energy," a "life" or "vigor," positive, forceful words which evoke the sorts of qualities we would *like* a state to have. Similarly, when he regarded the commoners who dominated the French National Assembly, he wondered, "Who could flatter himself that these men, suddenly, and as it were by enchantment, snatched from humblest

rank of subordination, would not be intoxicated with their unprepared greatness?"[38] It is difficult to resist the force of the charge,
and almost impossible to keep in mind the "as it were" amidst
"suddenly," "enchantment," "snatched," and "intoxicated."

Burke's anger and his rhetorical talent could sometimes combine
to produce extremely subtle images of the finest sort—that is, the
sort that did not appear to be images at all. In the *Reflections,* he
wrote, "The tenant-right of a cabbage-garden, a year's interest in
a hovel, the good-will of an ale-house or a baker's shop, the very
shadow of a constructive property, are more ceremoniously treated
in our Parliament than with you the oldest and most valuable landed
possessions, in the hands of the most respectable personages, or than
the whole body of the moneyed and commercial interest of your
country."[39] His metaphor exaggerated vastly to make the point.
Yet his furious denunciations of the revolution, the extreme and
absolute moral categories into which he organized the *Reflections,*
made it possible for him to pass this figure as a descriptive statement.

Burke's language was lovely because it was lively. Human juices
coursed through his sentences. His vocabulary was dynamic, and
therefore persuasive and memorable. Even where the thought was
banal, the words could be engaging: "In all mutations (if mutations
must be) the circumstance which will serve most to blunt the edge
of their mischief, and to promote what good may be in them, is,
that they should find us with our minds tenacious of justice and
tender of property."[40] Few writers have drawn more effectively upon
the energetic resources of English.

The Rewards of Burke

For all Burke's talent, there is still something astonishing in the
fact that so much of what he wrote continues to merit, and receive,
attention. For the last forty years of his life, his essays and published
speeches were written almost exclusively in response to events which
few readers of later generations could reconstruct accurately and in
detail. It probably crossed his mind to write for posterity toward
the end, in such works as the *Reflections, An Appeal from the New to
the Old Whigs,* and *A Letter to a Noble Lord;* mostly, however, he
wrote to persuade the living.

The continuing appeal of Burke resides only in part in the importance of the events that made him write. The American and

French revolutions were obviously of major significance, but that alone does not account for the interest two centuries later in what Burke thought about them. There was little of intrinsic moment in the Hastings case, which in retrospect has all the earmarks of what the late twentieth century would call a "media event." Would we pay it much attention if Burke had not? Neither have campaign speeches been a staple in the diet of those who feed regularly upon the classics of modern literature.

Similarly, Burke's prose, while often magnificent, cannot alone account for why we read it. At its best, it was marvelously compendious, masterfully balanced, full of delightful surprises, grandly cadenced, punctuated with illuminating figures. Yet Burke was not above monotony (as any reader will discover who takes on the several volumes of Hastings speeches), verbal tricks, or simply bullying the reader—as in much of what he wrote on the French Revolution.

What Burke wrote is worth reading because his vision is worth sharing. It was personal, although not precisely unique; it was coherent, although not perfectly consistent; it was concrete, vivid, wholly human and therefore universal; and while commonly political and contemporary, it was charged with moral import.

It is difficult to mistake Burke for anyone else, to imagine that anyone else could have written what he did. His ideas were traditional, but shaped within the special mold of his mind and experience. Decidedly minor works, familiar to few but specialists, still bear his distinctive mark:

I do not vilify theory and speculation: no, because that would be to vilify reason itself. . . . No,—whenever I speak against theory, I mean always a weak, erroneous, fallacious, unfounded, or imperfect theory; and one of the ways of discovering that it is a false theory is by comparing it with practice. This is the true touchstone of all theories which regard man and the affairs of men,—Does it suit his nature in general?—does it suit his nature as modified by his habits?[41]

Burke fashioned a public literary voice, but it was a convention and not a mask. There is no doubting that his pronouncements were deeply felt; the passion and conviction of his personal views were in most of them—and, interestingly enough, in much of his private correspondence as well.

In almost anything he wrote, it is difficult to go far without coming upon some of his central commitments. Whether he was dealing with the constitution, empire, revolution, economics, or history, he was at bottom dealing with his vision of history, human nature, and morality. Emphasis shifted, but the coherence is impressive. Moreover, whatever the subject, it was in human scale. Burke was a religious man, but he knew few ways to condemn an idea more roundly than to call it "metaphysical." He despised abstractions, and though like all men he could not avoid them, still his preference afforded wide purchase to what he wrote: "The excellence of mathematics and metaphysics is, to have but one thing before you; but he forms the best judgment in all moral disquisitions who has the greatest number and variety of considerations in one view before him, and can take them in with the best possible consideration of the middle results of all."[42]

It is easy to share the company of a mind which seeks to charm, fascinate, enlighten, impress. It can be less comfortable to spend much time with Burke, since—although he sought all those effects from time to time—he insistently and almost compulsively raised questions of right and wrong. His work could run to preachiness, but more often there was a winning earnestness seeking to remind us that life was consequential, that behavior had moral implications, that we were responsible for our actions, that—whether or not we knew it or desired it—what we did mattered. This Burke commands heed, and rewards it.

Chapter Three

The British Constitution

The Roots of Conflict

The British constitution was no single document, in the manner of the American and French constitutions of the late eighteenth century. Rather, it was a collection of laws, charters, parliamentary declarations, judicial decisions, and customary practices. Collectively and over time, they had come to define the jurisdictions, prerogatives, and interrelationships of institutions and the rights and duties of those persons governed by them. As a result, the constitution was subject to a wide variety of fine interpretations which may have created a certain fuzziness on numerous points. Toward the end of the seventeenth century, however, events clarified some central matters.

In 1685, after two generations of conflict which had even erupted into civil war, James II acceded to the throne. Englishmen thus found themselves with a monarch who regarded his prerogatives with disturbing expansiveness and who justified them in terms which sounded distinctly like an argument from divine right. To make matters worse, James was a Roman Catholic in a nation where anti-Catholic prejudice sometimes reached hysterical proportions. While the king had his supporters (Tories) among the great landed families who dominated Parliament, the same social stratum also produced vigorous opponents (Whigs) who were inclined to see a vast royal prerogative as threatening to the long-standing liberties of his subjects. It is significant, however, that the king's excesses—actual or feared—became sufficiently alarming to drive Whigs and even certain Tories into a coalition which forced James II to flee the throne and the country in 1688.

His successors, King William III and Queen Mary II, who ruled jointly, were not put firmly in place without certain constitutional adjustments. In the course of 1688–89, a number of parliamentary

decisions which became known collectively as the Revolution Settlement definitively established the supremacy of Parliament over
the throne, although powers of considerable scope were still left in
royal hands. Governments were still appointed and dismissed by,
and responsible to, the crown (though it came to be accepted that
they also had to have the support of Parliament). But while the
monarchy still ruled, at least in part, the Revolution Settlement
established that Parliament would set the terms of that rule and
define the limitations upon it. For example, the religion of the
monarch could not henceforth be Roman Catholic.

By the middle of the eighteenth century, it was plain that nearly
all political persuasions had come, though perhaps with varying
degrees of enthusiasm, to accept the Revolution Settlement. Certain
differences did remain, especially when it came to interpreting what
had happened in 1688. In one view, a Papist clique at the court,
treasonable by its intimate association with the Roman Catholic
monarchy of arch-rival France, had attempted to subvert the constitution and return to the absolutism of darker times. The Revolution had simply brought the constitution back into congruence
with traditional practices and restored ancient liberties which the
Stuart dynasty had schemed into disuse. For others, the English
crown, surely the central component of the constitutional complex,
had been emasculated by a conspiracy of great Whig families who
wished to turn the monarch into their own private puppet while
they dominated the great offices of state, as they had for so much
of the first half of the eighteenth century.

But these were rhetorical conflicts over an increasingly distant
past. By the mid-eighteenth century, the labels "Whig" and "Tory"
barely referred to any existing political reality, and certainly not to
the poles of an ideological spectrum or even mutually exclusive
position. The great blocs of years gone by had long since splintered
internally. Individuals passed easily from group to group; different
groups found themselves allied on one issue, at odds on the next.
Entirely separate clutches of parliamentarians each took the label of
Whig, often for sentimental reasons, so that it became difficult to
say what the word meant. Meanwhile, hardly more than a handful
of incorrigible nostalgics would answer to the name of Tory. Day-
to-day policy rather than the constitution itself became the focus of
politics, which in its turn was becoming more fluid as it drained
of ideology. The Revolution Settlement defined a framework within

which everyone would operate. Moreover, social background reinforced this broad consensus. Whigs and Tories and their eighteenth-century successors alike were all dominated by the landed elite, whose material interests and social circumstances tended to promote a roughly common world view.

This relatively stable situation was particularly agreeable to the various and only loosely linked Whiggish groups which came steadily to dominate the ministries of George II's reign, stretching from 1727 to 1760. In control of an administration, a few men did not merely set policy. They could also enjoy and dispense the generous emoluments which often accompanied office. Few politicians rated any component of power higher than that of patronage. Drawing on a seemingly endless list of archaic sinecures—the burdens weighing upon the King's Taster of Wines in Dublin were not intolerable—a government might sustain and even enlarge its power by attaching to itself ambitious men of purchasable loyalties. By the standards of a later age, such practices were corrupt. Indeed, even in the eighteenth century itself, every group was at one time or another charged with seeking nothing more than a comfortable proximity to the royal treasury. However, wholly functional offices also carried handsome perquisites, and holders of sinecures sometimes performed important administrative tasks while utterly ignoring the laughable formal charges of their position. As a general rule, people accepted the notion that public service merited reward from public funds. Politicians merely exploited this situation to supplement family connections, personal friendships, and programmatic affinities with material ties.

Whig beneficiaries of these arrangements were understandably reluctant to relinquish the advantages which had accrued to them thanks to George II's habit of drawing governments from their ranks. But relinquish they did, not long after the expiration of their royal patron and the accession of his grandson, George III. What happened then was entirely consistent with the workings of English politics, however little consolation that was to the great Whig families— the Pelhams, the Cavendishes, the Russells—whose influence was now sharply curtailed. As George II's long reign had worn on, it became clear that he was not about to swerve in his loyalties to the Whigs. For ambitious men out of office, the one ray of sunshine was that the king's life, like all things, would one day come to an end. It followed that cultivation of his successor might repay the effort. The future George III eventually found himself surrounded with a circle of friends whose admiration and dedication may possibly have been warmed by the hope of future preferment.

When George embarked upon his reign of sixty years, it was perfectly natural that he would bestow favor upon his friends, who are more accurately seen simply as men long excluded from office than as anything approaching latter-day Tories. The most notable— in Whig circles the word was "notorious"—of the new king's favorites was his former tutor and later closest confidant, the Earl of Bute. With little political experience, he rapidly found his way to a seat in the cabinet and shortly thereafter to the eminence of the First Lord of the Treasury. Such abrupt ascendancy was unusual, but in principle it scarcely differed from the politics of the Whig supremacy: Bute had a well-placed friend.

Bute's ministry did not last long—he had no solid base in Parliament—but he retained the king's ear and was widely supposed in Whig circles to have a decisive say in George's choice of governments and the royal dispensation of sinecures. In the ensuing years, the Rockingham Whigs held office for a year in 1765–66 and other Whig combinations had a brief fling. But the king did succeed in separating the great Whig families from the sustained monopoly of patronage and thus decisively broke their grip on political power. His success was not, as many Whigs thought, an assertion of new royal prerogative so much as a demonstration of how much influence the Revolution Settlement had left in the hands of a monarch ready to use it. George III was merely determined to have his own people around him, and not his grandfather's; the Whigs could not keep from seeing something sinister in it all.

Such suspicions drew sustenance also from the government's behavior in the uproarious Wilkes case.[1] John Wilkes came into English politics and political journalism from the background of a newly wealthy commercial family. His newspaper, the *North Briton,* often spoke a language which struck responsive chords among the mercantile interests in those provincial towns whose growth and prosperity were heavily dependent upon overseas trade. In 1763, George III was apparently moving in a direction that would reverse the policy of imperial expansion; accordingly, the *North Briton* flayed the monarch in terms even more inflammatory than it customarily employed. The king and his supporters wanted a libel action at the very least and though Wilkes was a member of Parliament, they were able to apply massive pressure and extract a vote which canceled his immunity from prosecution.

Wilkes was able to win one significant legal battle. He had been arrested originally under a blanket warrant which did not name him specifically; government attorneys defended the action by pleading reasons of state, but the courts overruled them. Wilkes still faced criminal charges; before they had been resolved, he went off to France for what probably he had intended to be only a brief respite. Pleasures of the flesh distracted him, however, and it was 1768 before he returned to run once more for Parliament. His defiance of the government made him a popular figure; technically an outlaw, he carried a strong majority in a riotous election in Middlesex, to the delight of certain middle-class strata and of urban workingmen aggrieved by a nagging economic crisis. When the government went ahead and pressed charges, which included seditious libel and blasphemy, Wilkes ended up with a sentence of twenty-two months in prison—and became even more the focus for popular protest against authority.

While Whigs had no sympathy with Wilkes's provocative style or the tumult he was occasioning in the towns, they could hardly stand silent at the government's next move. Bent on teaching Wilkes and his type a lesson, the king and his ministers pressed Parliament to revoke his election in Middlesex. After exerting every ounce of influence at their disposal, they succeeded in February 1769. Two weeks later, Wilkes's constituents reelected him; Parliament unseated him the following day. Electorate and legislature defied one another again in March, and yet again in April, when the Commons finally seated Wilkes's opponent, who had captured a miserable handful of votes.

Whig aristocrats and a rascal like Wilkes made strange company. What gentleman wished to defend a man who lashed volatile urban crowds into a fury with his attacks upon the docility of a corrupt Parliament while amusing himself on the side by writing lascivious poetry? As a cause, Wilkes the man was an embarrassment, but the issues embodied in his case were inescapable. There was the possibility that the hounding of Wilkes might deter any legitimate criticism of government; the integrity of elections and the independence of Parliament seemed to be at stake. When the Rockingham Whigs viewed the Wilkes case in conjunction with their misgivings about the crown's patronage, the influence of the king's

circle, and the implications of it all for royal prerogative, they began
to conclude that they had a crisis of serious magnitude on their
hands. It was Burke who gave voice to their concern.

Crown and Constitution

Thoughts on the Cause of the Present Discontents appeared in the
summer of 1770, its publication delayed somewhat by Burke's extreme care in revising and polishing it. For it was "an undertaking
of some degree of delicacy"—though not, as he claimed, because
it was unlikely to please everyone. The delicacy arose because Burke
was firing not simply another salvo in the interminable pamphlet
war of English politics. Instead, he was about to raise some fundamental constitutional questions—never an enterprise to be taken
lightly or conducted clumsily.

Burke's enumeration of the discontents was a model of the serial
sentence flavored with the spice of political hyperbole:

That government is at once dreaded and contemned; that the laws are
despoiled of all their respected and salutary terrors; that their inaction is
a subject of ridicule, and their exertion of abhorrence; that rank, and office
and title, and all the solemn plausibilities of the world, have lost their
reverence and effect; that our foreign politics are as much deranged as our
domestic economy; that our dependencies are slackened in their affection,
and loosened from their obedience; that we know neither how to yield nor
how to enforce; that hardly anything above or below, abroad or at home,
is sound and entire; but that disconnection and confusion, in offices, in
parties, in families, in Parliament, in the nation, prevail beyond the
disorders of any former time: these are facts universally admitted and
lamented.[2]

After dismissing other explanations for these problems, Burke pro-
ceeds directly to the question which had been nagging Whigs for
a decade. "The power of the crown," he wrote, "almost dead and
rotten as Prerogative, has grown up anew, with much more strength,
and far less odium, under the name of Influence."[3]

In order to slough off the restraints placed upon the throne by
the Revolution Settlement and *"to secure to the court the unlimited and
uncontrolled use of its own vast influence, under the sole direction of its own
private favor . . . ."* a three-part plan had been formulated.[4] First,
the court would seek not to dominate, but to isolate itself from,

the ministry so that it might form a second, secret, and irresponsible ministry of its own. Then this court ministry, working against the regularly appointed one, would both make policy and hoard the emoluments of government. Finally, Parliament was to be divided and degraded, paralyzed into acquiescence in the whole scheme.

Burke was careful not to lay the blame for this plan upon the king himself. Rather, it was the work of a "cabal" which had insidiously wormed its way into his favor and now exploited the vast resources for influence which he commanded. The "cabal" momentarily shattered the reputation of the Whigs with a slanderous and hypocritical campaign against "corruption," thus depriving the people at large of their familiar and trusted leaders. Then it prepared to fill the void in government itself, but indirectly, by means of the nefarious court ministry. Meanwhile, it missed no opportunity to defame and to fragment any possible opposition.

Burke took special exception to one particular attempt by the "cabal" to discredit its critics. The opposition, it had been claimed, was in the thrall of an aristocarcy seeking an undue influence of its own. Burke answered flatly that the peers were men of property and that property meant power: the two never should and never could be divorced. Individual nobles, on the other hand, owed such influence as they had to public favor and approval. It was in this passage that Burke made his oft-quoted remark, "I am no friend to aristocracy, in the sense at least in which that word is usually understood. If it were not a bad habit to moot cases on the supposed ruin of the constitution, I should be free to declare, that if it must perish, I would rather by far see it resolved into any other form, than lost in that austere and insolent domination."[5] He has widely, and mistakenly, been taken to have meant that he held no brief for that social order. But Burke's reference was plainly to a form of government. Far from seeing any dangers in the legitimate political ambitions of the nobility, he was disappointed that more peers had not set themselves against "a backstairs influence and clandestine government."[6] Burke was not being neutral to aristocracy; rather, he was describing the deterioration of its proper constitutional role as a countervailing force against the royal prerogative.

The system which Burke called the "double cabinet," or the "exterior and interior administrations," where the court ministry confused and frustrated the designs of the regular ministry while proceeding to make policy itself free from parliamentary scrutiny, was bound to call the Earl of Bute immediately to mind. But Burke had no desire to load all the national distempers on the shoulders of one man. He first singled out Bute by name, then rather disingenuously absolved him of most responsibility and clearly implied a much larger faction was at work to infuse "a *system of favoritism*" into the government.

It was no security against this threat that England had a government of laws, since the laws "reach but a very little way" and left ample discretion to their executors. When a minister with such latitude could demonstrate his worthiness of the public trust, then there was no cause for alarm. It was otherwise, however, with the "interior administration":

> That man who before he comes into power has no friends, or who coming into power is obliged to desert his friends, or who losing it has no friends to sympathize with him; he who has no sway among any part of the landed or commercial interest, but whose whole importance has begun with his office, and is sure to end with it, is a person who ought never to be suffered by a controlling Parliament to continue in any of those situations which confer the lead and direction of all our public affairs; because such a man has no connection with the interest of the people.[7]

But the problem was that there was no longer a "controlling Parliament." The constitution prescribed that Parliament's "first duty" was to oppose governments which lacked popular confidence or which were dominated by unpopular court factions. The king chose the ministers; the Parliament could choose not to support them. But with the opposition scattered and dispirited, and the "interior cabinet" beyond Parliament's reach, such control was difficult to exercise. It was no small matter: without that control, "everything is lost, Parliament and all."[8] By "all," Burke meant nothing less than the constitution itself.

The Wilkes case was Burke's most specific instance of what he saw as the evisceration of Parliament, or at least the House of Commons. "The virtue, spirit, and essence of a House of Commons consists in its being the express image of the feelings of the nation. It was not instituted to be a control *upon* the people, as of late it has been taught by a doctrine of the most pernicious tendency. It was designed as a control *for* the people."[9] By "the people," it is worth noting, Burke did not mean every British man, woman, and child. Rather, his reference was to the electorate—whose size he some years later estimated at perhaps 400,000 men, and whose franchise was in large part determined by the ownership of property. Far from being the *demos*, his "people" were very much an elite, and he could therefore be comfortable in arguing that it was preferable for the Commons to reflect every whim and caprice of the "populace" thus conceived than to fall utterly out of touch with its constituency. Yet what had happened in the Wilkes case but a successful effort by the "cabal" to sever the connection between opinion and representation?

Burke refused, however, to believe that the "king's friends" set after Wilkes merely for his own sake. Wilkes was to be an example to the opposition, since the resolution of the case showed that popular support was no sure road to political success. Indeed, "Popularity was to be rendered, if not directly penal, at least highly dangerous." Critics of the government would now think twice: "Resistance to power has shut the door of the House of Commons to one man; obsequiousness and servility, to none."[10]

The difficulty was that much of the popular furor over the voiding of Wilkes's elections was directed at the House of Commons. But while the House had cast the votes which kept Wilkes out, Burke was intent upon directing attention back at the real villain: "But we must purposely shut our eyes, if we consider this matter merely as a contest between the House of Commons and the electors. The true contest is between the electors of the kingdom and the crown; the crown acting by an instrumental House of Commons."[11] The crown had been able to make the House its instrument because of the extensive sinecures and discretionary funds which were at the royal disposal under the general rubric of the Civil List. Parliament's real error lay in its failure to keep a closer check upon this immense source of influence, one which Burke implied had been used to corrupt Parliament itself and turn it into "the best appendage and support of arbitrary power that ever was invented by the wit of man."[12]

To the modern reader, it may seem curious that Burke's indictment of royal influence stopped abruptly at this point. He had made his case, however, and had been careful to criticize a "cabal" rather than a king; there was no advantage in giving the impression that he was accusing the occupant of the throne. Indeed, when it came to making some concluding recommendations, Burke turned his gaze back upon the same Parliament which he had just argued was not basically at fault, save for its lack of scrupulosity in examining and approving monies for the Civil List.

Given the heat of his charges, Burke's treatment of proposed remedies prompt both surprise and some insight into how gingerly he approached constitutional change. He had described the history of a disease, he said, but he had little to say about a cure. He rejected the idea of reducing the duration of Parliaments from seven to three years in hope that the Commons would be more readily accountable to their constituents. More frequent elections, he feared, would only play into the hands of the crown with its substantial funds for influencing the vote. Moreover, and here he no doubt had the Middlesex disorders in mind, Burke had reservations about any measure which would increase public tumult in the towns at election time. Equally, he could not support a place-bill—that is, legislation which would bar from Parliament the holder of a sinecure or other royal gratuity. Placemen were widely supposed to be purchased men, sure votes when the ministry came to toting up a division. Burke was concerned, however, that certain legitimate interests—for instance, military officers who held their commissions from the king— might be excluded from Parliament in the process, and he was rarely willing to eliminate an evil if he canceled out something good in the bargain. Besides, to prohibit placemen from seats was to strike at a visible form of influence, one which was relatively open. If the existing practice were nullified, Burke feared that the crown would only resort to less conspicuous but equally effective forms of influence which he did not specify yet by their very evasiveness, might be more difficult to counteract. Again, it is the utilitarian Burke at work, mindful of shortcomings in the way things operate, but apprehensive about the impact of the cure: "It is no inconsiderable part of wisdom, to know how much of an evil ought to be tolerated; lest, by attempting a degree of purity impracticable in degenerate times and manners, instead of cutting off the subsisting ill-practices, new corruptions might be produced for the concealment and security of the old."[13]

What Burke did suggest was rhetorically more radical and constitutionally less disruptive than either of these measures. If the "cabal," with its access to crown revenues, had manipulated Parliament, if it had corrupted Parliament out of its proper responsiveness to popular opinion, then Burke urged action not against the buyers but the bought. Considering where things stood, "I see no other way for the preservation of a decent attention to public interest in the representatives, but *the interposition of the body of the people itself. . . ."*[14] It is important to understand that this was no call for rebellion, no Lockian assertion that government had broken the political contract with society, which could now take matters into its own hands. Burke meant that "the people"—again, his term for the electorate—could no longer trust members of the House of Commons to reflect the popular view or expect that they would set themselves straight without prodding. It was up to the voters to examine incumbents' records more carefully, to set more systematic standards of parliamentary conduct, to guard against government manipulation of elections, and thus to help rid the Commons of those yea-sayers to power. ("He that supports every administration subverts all government.")[15] The "cabal" would have a harder time of it without an acquiescent Parliament. In sum, Burke was asking "the people" to do what the constitution fully permitted them to do, but what Burke was implying they had never had the need to do during the generation prior to 1760.

His second suggestion was something more of a departure. The "cabal," he charged, had tried to throw opposition into disarray by preaching that all political parties were by their nature divisive and fractious—though the "cabal" itself was nothing if not a "court party." By keeping potential critics atomized, the "king's friends" obviously forestalled concerted resistance to their policies. What Burke failed to note here, but surely knew, was that impugning the idea of party was a vein of the purest orthodoxy in eighteenth-century English politics. Party had long since been synonymous with faction, clique, a group of schemers who stood not within but against the unified national ranks, who sought not to advance the common good but detach a share of it for their private gain. Much of this was simply talk, an accepted way of blackening one's opponents. Besides, by the middle of the century it was increasingly plain that parties were there to stay—an ineradicable evil. Something in the human makeup, or perhaps in the nature of politics, seemed inexorably and inevitably to create them. The image of grasping factions persisted, though behind it there was developing a kind of grudging tolerance of what then passed for parties—even if, by 1770, it had yet to build itself up into frank approval.

At the conclusion of *Thoughts on the Cause of the Present Discontents,* Burke sought to give members of the fractured parliamentary op-

position some basis for reuniting against the crown's offensive, and
that basis was party. In part, he argued, party was a vital defensive
mechanism for an opposition on the run. By pooling their information and intelligence, individuals could alert one another to danger earlier; by pooling their influence, they could resist it more
effectively. Men of little standing could count for something in a
party; outside one, "the greatest talents are unserviceable to the
public." There was no other way: "When bad men combine, the
good must associate; else they will fall, one by one, an unpitied
sacrifice in a contemptible struggle."[16]

Burke was not content, however, to let the argument rest there,
since it made of party a creature of necessity, born of crisis only
and probably doomed to extinction once the crisis had passed. A
merely defensive conception of party fit the orthodox view, and
indeed it was a view which Burke had stated the year before in a
polemical pamphlet, *Observations on a Late Publication, Intituled "The
Present State of the Nation"*: "Party division, whether on the whole
operating for good or evil, are things inseparable from free government. This is a truth which, I believe, admits little dispute, having
been established by the uniform experience of all ages."[17] But Burke
had gone on in the *Observations* to a more positive acceptance of
party, anticipating his position in the *Thoughts*. He described the
Rockingham Whigs as bound together not only by their social
position—though it was important that many of them were "of the
first families, and weightiest properties, in the kingdom"—but also
by their devotion to the constitution and their personal loyalty to
Rockingham himself, whom Burke characterized as a model of honor
and probity.

It was this unity, based upon principle, which Burke saw as the
value and strength of his party, and he suggested that any government which lacked it—meaning all George III's governments save
that of 1765–66—was bound to reflect its disunity in its policy.
Burke assailed coalitions which purported to heal political divisions
but really only guaranteed discord within the administration: "Nor
will the mind of our sovereign ever know repose, his kingdom
settlement, or his business order, efficiency, or grace with his people,
until things are established upon the basis of some set of men, who
are trusted by the public, and who can trust one another."[18] In flat
contradiction of the prevalent notion that government ought to be
preserved *from* party, Burke was proposing that government ought

to be turned over *only to* a party—properly conceived, which is to say in the manner of the Rockingham Whigs.

In the *Thoughts,* Burke admitted that parties had had their ill effects on occasion. But he insisted that they were as natural a part of a commonwealth as families, "and we may as well affirm, that our natural regards and ties of blood tend inevitably to make men bad citizens, as that the bonds of our party weaken those by which we are held to our country."[19] He recalled the palmy days of Queen Anne, during whose reign (1702–1714)—"one of the most fortunate periods of our history"—England "was governed by a connection." The leaders of that great Whig party, men like Sunderland, Godolphin, Somers, and Marlborough, "believed that no men could act with effect, who did not act in concert."[20]

"Party is a body of men united for promoting by their joint endeavors the national interest upon some particular principle in which they are all agreed."[21] In a single paragraph which began with that famous sentence, Burke proceeded to make the succinct statement of party for which the whole work is best remembered. A politician who takes his own views seriously will attempt to realize them in public policy; he will become "the philosopher in action." In the case of parties, they will attempt to give effect to their principles by contending for those offices which make policy. In that competition, they will not completely proscribe other parties, but "they are bound to give to their own party the preference in all things." The goal is not personal gain, but the triumph of certain principles, the enactment of party programs, and these can be achieved only when the whole party—and not a few for the sake of coalition politics—is offered power. The behavior of a party of honorable men will clearly distinguish itself from that of parties seeking only material reward, and thus dignify the concept of party itself.[22]

After a brief attack upon the charge that party membership is equivalent to servility—it cannot be, he said, if we make sure from the outset that we agree with our prospective companions about the general principles of government—Burke concluded the *Thoughts* on a peculiar note: "There is, however, a time for all things. It is not every conjuncture which calls with equal force upon the activity of honest men; but critical exigencies now and then arise; and I am mistaken, if this be not one of them."[23] At first glance, it appears that Burke has withdrawn from his advanced and unorthodox position on party to one which assigns it a role merely in crisis—the implication being that in normal times it was still something like a necessary evil. Perhaps this was Burke's intention. Or perhaps he feared that his somewhat controversial views on party would distract attention from the immediate problem at hand and that it was best to moderate those views slightly for tactical purposes. Certainly a careful reading of the whole passage on party reveals nothing to suggest that Burke did not believe its principles applicable to all sorts of political situations. Indeed, even in the paragraph beginning with the sentences quoted above, Burke seemed to say that party is liable to be disadvantageous only when it is "too late"—that is, only when the enemies of free government have become so powerful that they can virtually outlaw party and turn "connection" into conspiracy. Burke pleaded a special need for party during the time of crisis in which he wrote. But *what* he wrote appears to justify parties and party government in nearly all times.

The view of the British constitution which emerges from the *Thoughts* is not a novel one, and Burke would certainly have been disconcerted had any of the prominent members of his party who viewed the manuscript before publication thought so. Burke's constitutional ideas were designed as a restatement of the Revolution Settlement against which the designs of the "cabal" would stand out in sharp relief. Moreover, the *Thoughts* offered a descriptive analysis of English government, not the sort of rampant criticism in which the narrator of the *Vindication* had engaged. Burke saw the crown and the Houses of Commons and Lords each playing a vital role and doing so in a delicate interrelationship. Aggrandizement or abdication of responsibilities in any of these institutions was bound to upset the balance which was the chief characteristic of the constitution.

It was precisely for this reason that Burke's proposals for change were so subdued, even though the traditional constitution itself appeared in jeopardy. For the forces which kept the English polity in balance were extremely intricate. If an imbalance began to appear, it was vital to measure the corrective carefully: "Our constitution stands on a nice equipoise, with steep precipices and deep waters upon all sides of it. In removing it from a dangerous leaning towards one side, there may be a risk of oversetting it on the other."[24] Burke's intention was not to move forward to some new constitutional arrangement—he deeply distrusted the idea of "*perfect* satisfaction in government"—but to restore the old balance. To do so meant to give great property its due and necessary role in government, to remove Parliament from its subordination to the "interior ministry" and reestablish its intimate connection with popular opinion, and then to have Parliament resist the influence of the "king's friends" by organized party action. All his impulses told him to go *back* to a received heritage rather than forward into uncertain and untried arrangements.

Moreover, there were enemies besides the "cabal" in those deep waters above which the constitution perched so precariously. The *Thoughts* closed with the following sentence: "If other ideas should prevail, things must remain in their present confusion, until they are hurried into all the rage of civil violence, or until they sink into the dead repose of despotism."[25] There were limits, in other words, upon the "interposition of the body of the people." The Wilkesite agitation was no matter of polite admonitions to power. The events of 1769 had touched off some ugly riots in a number of towns, and Burke had no more desire to see government fall into the hands of a mob than he wished it to reside in the lap of Lord Bute. Consequently, it was doubly urgent that the balance be set right, lest government further incite those lower social strata whose participation in politics the constitution had never envisaged. Although Burke wished to draw as much political advantage as he could from the injustice done Wilkes, he was still convinced that democracy threatened England nearly as much as cabalistic tyranny.

Historians are generally agreed that Burke's panicky vision of the "cabal" grossly exaggerated both the facts, including most especially the extent of Bute's power, and the danger to the traditional constitution. They deny the existence of a "double cabinet" and attribute the weakness of regularly appointed ministries during the 1760s to George III's inability to find a combination which could command both his personal confidence and a majority in Parliament. Indeed, in the year 1770 itself the concept of an "interior" and an "exterior" ministry began to look a little shaky, for the king finally found that right combination. Lord North was its chief figure, and he governed with comfortable parliamentary support for twelve years.[26]

What is less often noted of the *Thoughts* is that it was much more than simply Burke's "treatise on party," even if that was its most original contribution. More important, it was his first and for twenty years his fullest treatment of the English constitution. For the next two decades, in his speeches and writings, he would largely elaborate the themes and refine the positions he had raised in 1770.

The Politics of Opposition

Burke returned to the issue of royal influence repeatedly over the following years. When a defendant was accused of libeling the government, the judge in the case ruled that the jury was to confine itself to deciding whether or not the defendant had published the material in question, while the judge himself would rule upon whether or not it was libelous. Although the decision seems to have been legally sound, Burke and other Whigs bemoaned its implications for free expression, since of course the crown appointed judges.[27] When the subject of shortening the duration of Parliaments came up again, Burke reiterated his arguments from the *Thoughts,* prominent among which was the insistence that more frequent elections allowed more, and not less, latitude for royal influence. Even when the main subject was colonial policy, he was able to work in a reference to the "low, pimping politics of a court."[28]

Burke's most important attack upon royal influence came in 1780, however, when he introduced the single most important piece of legislation of his entire parliamentary career. Its intent was to reduce influence by reducing the financial resources available to the king in the Civil List. The speech with which Burke introduced and justified his proposals was full of quotable verities about the need for economies in government and the virtues of frugality with public monies. But, as he confessed at the beginning, what was "uppermost" in his mind "was the reduction of that corrupt influence which is itself the perennial spring of all prodigality and of all disorder. . . ."[29] Even so, it was necessary to be cautious, and one passage of the speech is worth quoting at length in order to give a sense of Burke's temperamental conservatism:

. . . as it is the interest of government that reformation should be early, it is the interest of the people that it should be temperate. It is their interest, because a temperate reform is permanent, and because it has a principle of growth. Whenever we improve, it is right to leave room for a further improvement. It is right to consider, to look about us, to examine the effect of what we have done. Then we can proceed with confidence, because we can proceed with intelligence. Whereas in hot reformations, in what men more zealous than considerate call *making clear work,* the whole is generally so crude, so harsh, so indigested, mixed with so much imprudence and so much injustice, so contrary to the whole course of human nature and human institutions, that the very people who are most eager for it are among the first to grow disgusted at what they have done. Then some part of the abdicated grievance is recalled from its exile in order to become a corrective of the correction. Then the abuse assumes all the credit and popularity of a reform. The very idea of purity and disinterestedness in politics falls into disrepute, and is considered as a vision of hot and inexperienced men; and thus disorders become incurable, not by the virulence of their own quality, but by the unapt and violent nature of the remedies. A great part, therefore, of my idea of reform is meant to operate gradually: some benefits will come at a nearer, some at a more remote period. We must no more make haste to be rich by parsimony than by intemperate acquisition.[30]

The House of Commons may have taken Burke even more seriously than he wished: the version of his bill for "economical reform" which only became law two years later was not as severe with sinecures as Burke had proposed.

While ever watchful toward the influence of the court, Burke also remained alert to the residual impact of the Wilkesite agitation. In 1771, Burke was still flogging the Commons for having seated Wilkes's opponent two years earlier.[31] As the decade wore on, however, popular protest against the treatment of Wilkes began to generalize into various but persistent calls for reforming Parliament. To the old demand for triennial as opposed to septennial Parliaments the reformers joined various schemes for enlarging the suffrage and rearranging the basis for representation—which then vastly overrepresented southern England and rural areas in general at the expense of the north and newly developing urban centers. Although the reform movement of the 1770s was reasonably orderly, danger seemed to lurk in the expanding number of its adherents and its increasingly organized character. The idea of universal male suffrage, which was gathering some support, can only have sent shivers through a man like Burke, who could not dissociate the exercise of political responsibilities from the stabilizing ownership of property. Years earlier, Burke had even half seriously proposed *reducing* the electorate so as to minimize the practice of buying off the poorer voters.[32]

The violence which flared up in London during 1780 did little to improve the reputation of the reformists, even though the riots which held the city by the throat for days were in no way an outgrowth of the movement to overhaul Parliament. They were in part an expression of profound economic discontent among the poor, who took the occasion of some legislation which slightly loosened discriminations against Roman Catholics to vent their rage. The anti-Catholic fury of the mobs was wholly disconnected from the previous political agitation, and indeed Wilkes was instrumental in helping to bring the rioting to an end. But the sight of the *plebs* in uproar was a grim one for defenders of the established political order. In a speech of 1781, Burke denied that he had any untoward attachment to the aristocracy and even claimed that should the rich and powerful ever encroach upon "the smallest rights of the poorest people in the kingdom," he would oppose the aristocracy—by violence, if it came to that. On the other hand, and the riots of the previous year cannot have been far from his mind, Burke vowed that if "the poor and low and feeble" should ever come "to turn their liberty into a cloak for maliciousness, and to seek a privilege of exemption, not from power, but from the rules of morality and virtuous discipline, then I would join my hand to make them feel the force which a few united in a good cause have over a multitude of the profligate and ferocious."[33]

In a speech prepared for but never delivered to the Commons, Burke confronted the issue of parliamentary reform squarely.[34] He derided the claim that the reformers reflected any deep-seated urge for change in the electorate. Yet they were enough of a bother to elicit from him the prediction that their efforts must lead to nothing less than "the destruction of the Constitution" and "anarchy." He regretted that political discourse had foresaken its customary preoccupation with men and measures, and drifted instead into far more disturbing debates: "we are grown out of humor with the English Constitution itself. . . ."[35] What had been an object of pride was not only held up to criticism and contempt but, worse, was examined to see whether it "did or did not accord with a preconceived scheme in the minds of certain gentlemen." Burke would have none of it:

It is for fear of losing the inestimable treasure we have that I do not venture to game it out of my hands for the vain hope of improving it. I look with filial reverence on the Constitution of my country, and never will cut it in pieces, and put it into the kettle of any magician, in order to boil it, with the puddle of their compounds, into youth and vigor. On the contrary, I will drive away such pretenders; I will nurse its venerable age, and with lenient arts extend a parent's breath.[36]

Here Burke unleashed his first sustained offensive against the position that men—as discrete, individual human beings—had certain "natural rights," among which was the right to self-government. As for persons who argued thus, "it is ridiculous to talk to them of the British Constitution upon any or upon all of its bases: for they lay it down, that every man ought to govern, himself, and that, where he cannot go, himself, he must send his representative; that all other government is usurpation, and is so far from having a claim to our obedience, it is not only our right, but our duty, to resist it."[37]

No person pretended, said Burke, that the House of Commons, much less the House of Lords or the crown, were or were ever meant to be consistent with such a plan. These institutions functioned not in terms of "natural rights" but of "prior rights." It was a *prescriptive* constitution, "a constitution whose sole authority is, that it has existed time out of mind."[38]

By invoking prescription, Burke put himself in a wholly different conceptual world from the natural-rights theorists, and had as well sounded a note which had not appeared in the *Thoughts on the Cause of the Present Discontents,* though it was not new to his political thought. In Roman law, prescription was the principle to which one resorted in order to fend off investigations into one's right to certain properties. It denied the legitimacy of such inquiries if the current possessor of the property could prove current usage and the inquirer could not demonstrate recent usage.[39] How the property had been acquired by its current user became irrelevant. In terms of eighteenth-century English politics, crown, Lords, and Commons could prove lengthy "usage"—that is, they had performed something like their present roles "time out of mind," a concrete fact which rendered such abstract intrusions as natural rights irrelevant in their turn.

It can be argued that prescription is a fundamentally antihistorical principle, since its emphasis is upon usage and not upon how that usage came to be exercised in the first place.[40] Burke, however, had no wish to argue so. He was just as concerned to show the lineage of prevailing constitutional arrangements: "It is a presumption in favor of any settled scheme of government against any untried proj-

ect, that a nation has long existed and flourished under it."[41] The
constitution worked precisely because it had evolved *over time,* and
in response to real human conditions and not out of abstract speculation. It could be seen as a sort of "choice," but "not of one day
or one set of people, not a tumultuary and giddy choice; it is a
deliberate election of ages and of generations; it is a constitution
made by what is ten thousand times better than choice; it is made
by the peculiar circumstances, occasions, tempers, dispositions, and
moral, civil, and social habitudes of the people, which disclose
themselves only in a long space of time. It is a vestment which
accommodates itself to the body."[42] Such an arrangement was infinitely superior to whatever might be fashioned by the individual
human mind in any given moment: "The individual is foolish, the
multitude, for the moment, is foolish, when they act without de-
liberation; but the species, it almost always acts right."[43]

Prescription was not a doctrine whose sanction Burke used only
against the reformers. It protected the constitution and its citizens
from royal intrusions upon ancient rights as well. In early 1768,
the Earl of Bute's son-in-law had challenged the title to certain
hereditary possessions held by the Duke of Portland, a member of
the Rockingham connection. Political considerations were involved,
since control of the territories in question entailed control of their
parliamentary seats, but Burke saw even more at stake. He argued
that prescription sanctioned the duke's rights of property, that long
family possession protected them against challenge to title, and he
helped draft legislation to that effect. The next year, a bill passed
which legalized the employment of prescription against the crown
if it attempted to question title to property held more than sixty
years.[44]

One central concern of the *Thoughts* had been the necessity of
Members of Parliament maintaining a close congruence with "public
opinion." Yet, as it soon became clear, Burke by no means wished
to argue that any representative ought to be the captive of his
particular constituency. The individual member's relationship to
public opinion turned out to be rather more intricate.

In 1774, Burke had the opportunity to move from the seat for
little Wendover to one for Bristol, an important commercial city
and port for overseas trade. Once the election was over, the other
successful candidate for Bristol's two seats promised to comport
himself in Parliament strictly according to the wishes of his con-

stituents. Burke had a somewhat different position. While he expected to stay in the closest possible communication with his
constituents, Burke informed them—in the sort of speech which
perhaps a prudent man delivers after and not before an election—
that they had elected his judgment and his conscience rather than
his obedience. The constitution, he claimed, knew nothing of binding instructions from constituents to their representative. For no
one constituency was identical with the entire nation, and it was
the interest of the whole which Members of Parliament were du-
tybound to serve. Bristol must not be surprised if the good of
England, or of the even larger empire, demanded that Burke vote
contrary to Bristol's wishes.[45]

This argument, standard for the time, was also something of a
refinement upon Burke's position in the *Thoughts*. It relaxed somewhat the close correspondence of views between representative and
represented for which he had called there, or at least it recast the
notion of public opinion in more general terms. It conferred substantial independence upon the members and demanded a broad
exercise of discretion and reason on their part—which was exactly
why Burke thought Parliament ought to be reserved for men prepared for and experienced in public responsibilities, which was to
say men of property.

As it turned out, the Bristol electorate was not entirely enamored
of these notions. Burke was a conscientious representative, and he
ran numerous favor-seeking errands into the labyrinth of government
for individual constituents. But he spent little time in Bristol, and
on several important occasions voted directly contrary to the wishes
of the majority there. These votes did not go unnoticed, and when
Burke ran for reelection in 1780 he was plainly on the defensive.
"Look Gentlemen, to the *whole* tenor of your member's conduct,"
he implored an audience in the city in September. Voters who wished
an effective representative must allow him his integrity: "Depend
upon it, that the lovers of freedom will be free. . . . If we degrade
and deprave their minds by servility, it will be absurd to expect
that they who are creeping and abject towards us will ever be bold
and incorruptible assertors of our freedom against the most seducing
and the most formidable of all powers."[46] Burke went on to justify
his controversial votes at length, but within a few days he could
sense that he had failed to persuade many. Therefore, he withdrew

from the campaign, later securing a safe seat in the borough of Malton which was in the control of Lord Rockingham.

One of the several issues upon which the electors of Bristol had balked was Burke's support of the Roman Catholic relief bill of 1778. That act had done nothing to put Catholics in possession once more of the civil rights stripped from them nearly a century before. It had, however, removed the criminal penalties which bore upon Catholic clergy who undertook sacramental functions and upon Catholic teachers, and it also permitted Catholics to buy and to inherit land provided they swore a list of oaths to George III and against the House of Stuart and the temporal influence of the Pope within England. The act applied to England and Wales only, but Parliament soon passed additional legislation designed to extend similar relief to Irish Catholics. Anti-Catholicism ran deep in Bristol, as Burke well knew, and he was careful to keep his considerable role in preparing the relief bill inconspicuous. In 1780, however, he refused to deny his support of it and lectured his audience on the virtues of religious toleration.

The role of religion was the one important constitutional question which had not come up in the *Thoughts,* although Burke addressed himself to it more than once in the ensuing decade. Since the Church of England was an established church, supported by public monies, its clergy appointed by the government, it was manifestly part of the constitutional structure. The arrangement was relatively simple: ". . . the constitution has thought proper to take a security that the tax raised on the people shall be applied only to those who profess such doctrines and follow such a mode of worship as the legislature, representing the people, has thought most agreeable to their general sense,—binding, as usual, the minority, not to an assent to the doctrines, but to a payment of the tax."[47] The Church was free in many respects, though the legislature took care that it did not rise "far above the State" and develop "into that species of independency which it has been the great principle of our policy to prevent."[48] While parliamentary supremacy was thus beyond question, Burke would make certain that the established church was maintained with all due generosity:

There ought to be a symmetry between all the parts and orders of a state. A *poor* clergy in an *opulent* nation can have little correspondence with the body it is to instruct, and it is a disgrace to the public sentiments of religion. Such irreligious frugality is even bad economy, as the little that is given is entirely thrown away. Such an impoverished and degraded clergy in quiet times could never execute their duty, and in time of disorder would infinitely aggravate the public confusions.[49]

These sentiments were unexceptionable in their time. Where Burke went beyond many loyal Anglicans was in the rigor of his commitment to religious toleration: "If ever there was anything to which, from reason, nature, habit, and principle, I am totally averse, it is persecution for conscientious difference in opinion."[50] Fortunately, the constitution provided considerable latitude; it compelled no one to belong to the established church (though everyone had to pay for it, and certain civil disabilities still clung to non-Anglicans). There were numerous dissenting denominations in which nonconformists could freely and legally worship, and if none of those suited their tastes, they could create their own church, provided they could fund it themselves. Yet Burke would go further still, and build into the very constitutional fabric of the establishment a formal toleration which would sweep away most of the nagging discrimination still practiced: "Zealous as I am for the principle of an establishment, so just an abhorrence do I conceive against whatever may shake it. I know nothing but the supposed necessity of persecution that can make an establishment disgusting. I would have toleration a part of establishment, as a principle favorable to Christianity, and as a part of Christianity."[51]

Legalized discrimination, Burke contended, was generally admitted to be bad, and even when the laws were not strictly enforced they still had the effect of terrorizing dissenters. Moreover, nonenforcement was fundamentally capricious; one could not be confident that future magistrates might not seek to reapply bad laws if it suited their political purposes. Obviously, then, such laws ought to be struck down, in the interests not of the established church but of religion, since, "The cause of the Church of England is included in that of religion, not that of religion in the Church of England."[52] *All* conscientious religions ought to be tolerated, for to do otherwise was to forget that the real enemy was not a rival faith but the absence of faith:

Even the man who does not hold revelation, yet who wishes that it were proved to him, who observes a pious silence with regard to it, such a man, though not a Christian, is governed by religious principles. Let him be tolerated in this country. Let it be but a serious religion, natural or revealed, take what you can get. Cherish, blow up the slightest spark: one day it may be a pure and holy flame. By this proceeding you form an alliance offensive and defensive against those great ministers of darkness in the world who are endeavoring to shake all the works of God established in order and beauty.[53]

For the most part, Burke's arguments in favor of toleration and the removal of legal penalties upon non-Anglicans were utilitarian: religion would be stronger, English society more harmonious in a tolerant atmosphere. Yet he also spoke as though he obeyed higher dictates than prudence and convenience. Later in life, he would extend to religion the same protection as property and government enjoyed. All the principal religions of Europe, he argued in 1795, were *"prescriptive* religions. They have all stood long enough, to make prescription, and its train of legitimate prejudices, their main stay."[54] But even while defending his support of the Catholic relief bill before the Bristol electors in 1780, Burke put the matter also in terms of good and evil and referred to a high standard which would govern his conduct. Was toleration unpopular with the people? "No man carries further than I do the policy of making government pleasing to the people. But the widest range of this politic complaisance is confined within the limits of justice."[55] These words suggest that Burke did have a certain regard for "first principles," for eternal and immutable ideas of right and wrong which transcended human affairs. On occasion, he mixed his customary practical approach with his appeal to the "natural law" tradition. A few years earlier, when British power was unchallenged in the world, it might have been possible to tyrannize people on account of their religion with impunity. "But there is a revolution in our affairs, which makes it prudent to be just."[56] The invocation of compelling moral laws could also be entirely straightforward. To make it a crime to be a member of a group, religious or otherwise, he argued, "is an act of unnatural rebellion against the legal dominion of reason and justice; and this vice, in any constitution that entertains it, at one time or other will certainly bring on its ruin."[57]

There is no telling how Burke might have proceeded had he found the time or inclination to write a formal treatise on the constitution—something in the manner, say, of his *Philosophical Enquiry.*

As a professional politician, however, Burke dealt with political events as they arose; from the time he entered Parliament in 1766, everything he published was a *response* to some development. When it came to the English constitution, it is significant to note that Burke responded mainly to threats which would disturb that "nice equipoise." An ambitious court "cabal," an indolent Parliament sapped of its alertness to danger and corrupted into an indifference to its duties, a grasping judiciary, a mindless mob, abstract theories which blinded reformers to the awesome respect owed prescription, an electorate which would have its representative merely parrot its own caprices of the moment, religious bitterness born of unjust laws—any one of these could send tremors to the very foundations of the constitution. Burke was as much inclined to say that religious discrimination was an "evil" as to say that toleration was "good," to argue that party checked influence as that it promoted sound policy; in sponsoring the "economical reform," he proposed to *remove* certain offices of government.

Burke treated the constitution defensively. Its virtues were inherent; one perfected it—though Burke might have shunned the word—by preserving it, protecting it from intrusions and distortions. A politician of good sense, one who understood both the infinite complexity of government and the apparently inexhaustible human capacity for well-intentioned blundering about in it, would carry a standard which read: "Caution." His job was not to "make" the constitution viable, but to "keep" it viable, to avoid "extreme" measures of every sort, to do what was "right" by keeping others from doing what was "wrong."[58] Perhaps Burke came to these conclusions by reflection, perhaps by temperament. Or perhaps they arose from the mentality of parliamentary opposition, from the constant checking and resisting of a suspect power, even though Burke regarded such opposition as a positive act.

For all this, Burke could not be described as a man utterly satisfied with things as they were. Politics was always quest, rarely conquest. When the vocabulary of court "cabal" faded from Burke's lips, that of a corrupting court remained. Wilkes retired to a life of bourgeois pleasure in London; "democratic" reformers continued to abound. Some sinecures had been abolished; others remained. The established church had relaxed its grip upon outsiders; but Catholics and Protestant Dissenters alike were still something less than full citizens of the realm. All these lingering difficulties Burke saw as wrongs

to be righted and, because they distorted the constitution, as distempers that would throw its humors into imbalance.

But the constitution could be dislocated externally as well as
internally. The British Empire was an integral part of Burke's politics, and warrants separate examination in its own right.

Chapter Four
Constitution and Empire

When Burke entered politics in the 1760s, England (like every other nation on earth) was primarily a rural, agricultural society, the overwhelming majority of whose subjects drew their livelihood from working the land. Yet English prosperity, easily the most impressive in Europe, resulted not so much from the dramatic improvements in agricultural production which took place around the middle of the century as from a thriving and expansive overseas trade. Moreover, the vital components of this commerce were colonial possessions which sprawled across the globe from India to North America. An English politician ignorant of imperial affairs was approximately as useful as a physician who took no interest in the human circulatory system. Burke understood this fact; even before he assumed his political vocation, he had developed sufficient confidence in his knowledge of India, at least, that he was emboldened to debate none other than the formidable Dr. Johnson.[1]

The Imperial Constitution

The eighteenth-century empire had reached its zenith just before Burke developed his connection with the Marquis of Rockingham. The Seven Years War, concluded in 1763, delivered over to the English all North America east of the Mississippi, driving France from its holdings in both Canada and Louisiana (of which the latter fell to Spain). In the same conflict, the English had also largely evicted the French from India. Thereafter, England held relatively little territory on the subcontinent, but exercised enormous indirect influence through the East India Company, a government-chartered trading corporation which behaved much like a government itself.

Burke had no particular desire to expand this empire farther. Rather, he approached imperial questions as a student of good government, seeking to consolidate rather than to enlarge. Moreover, his location in the parliamentary opposition meant that he would not so much help govern the empire as criticize the administration's rule. When it came to America and to India, Burke attacked policy; only in the rather special case of Ireland did he help to shape it. Britain had acquired its empire by a variety of means, ranging from peaceful colonization to the unsqueamish use of force. The doctrine of prescription demanded, however, that Burke pay no mind to the means of acquisition: "When I first came into a public trust, I found your Parliament in possession of an unlimited legislative power over the colonies. I could not open the statute-book without seeing the actual exercise of it, more or less, in all cases whatsoever. This possession passed with me for a title. It does so in all human affairs. No man examines into the defects of his title to his estate or to his established government."[2] This analogy with the sanction Burke invoked for the English constitution was no coincidence, for alongside domestic institutional arrangements he saw standing a constitution of the British Empire, with Parliament at the head of each.[3] Within England, Parliament legislated and the executive power put its decisions into effect. Within the empire, Parliament's rule was more indirect. It operated through the legislatures of the various dependencies, "guides and controls them all without annihilating any."[4] Where these bodies could manage their own affairs, then the supreme Parliament kept its distance; where they could not, or where larger questions affecting the entire empire arose, or where conflicts of interest might develop, then "in order to enable Parliament to answer all these ends of provident and beneficient superintendence, her powers must be boundless."[5]

The scheme sounds simple, but Burke did not intend it to be so. Far from springing full-armored from the head of Zeus, the empire had grown up helter-skelter in several parts of the world. Modes of governance, degrees of subordination to the mother Parliament would differ from place to place and even time to time. "I never was wild enough to conceive that one method would serve for the whole, that the natives of Hindostan and those of Virginia could be ordered in the same manner, or that the Cutchery court and the grand jury of Salem could be regulated on a similar plan."[6] What remained uniform throughout, however, was English supremacy. Even if that boundless power were not to be exercised at all times, still it had to be recognized in principle, in case the need to use it ever arose, that Parliament ruled "as from the throne of heaven. . . ."[7]

It will bear special emphasis that Burke's conception of empire was not tyrannical. There were to be no doubts about the locus of ultimate sovereignty. But interest might frequently dictate a policy of keeping power in reserve, by resorting not to "watchful and suspicious government" but rather to colonial development through "a wise and salutary neglect. . . ."[8] Moreover, a supreme authority existed not only for cases of emergency or simply to give to the empire the unity which Burke found so necessary. In addition, Burke wished "to keep the whole body of this authority perfect and entire as I found it,—and to keep it so, not for our advantage solely, but principally for the sake of those on whose account all just authority exists: I mean the people to be governed."[9] His assumption was that in certain situations colonial governments might find it beyond their capacities to act effectively and would thus welcome the intervention of a competent power.

Plainly, Burke's vision of the imperial constitution was meant to be an analogue of the domestic version. In each he emphasized the prescriptive title to governance, the supremacy of Parliament, the reconciliation of "subordination and liberty."[10] There was a major flaw in the analogy, however. Within Britain, Parliament—or at least the House of Commons—was meant to be responsive to the interests of its constituency, the electorate. If Members of Parliament ever departed intolerably and unconstitutionally from voter opinion, then they might be turned out at election time—a version of the "interposition of the body of the people." Within the empire, the connection between Parliament and its constituents—whether these were conceived of as colonial legislatures or as *their* electors—was by no means so direct. No votes were cast overseas for elections to the imperial Parliament. At best, colonial legislatures could petition the superior institution, but there was no means of "interposition" within the law. The domestic constitution provided some counter-force to an irresponsible and insulated Parliament in the form of periodic elections; the imperial constitution provided none and thus leaned heavily upon the good will and good sense of the legislators at Westminster. It should perhaps not have surprised Burke of all people, with his healthy regard for human frailty, when so many of his fellow members proved fallible with respect to the American colonies and thus revealed the shortcomings in this theory of the imperial constitution.

This weakness in Burke's theory is evident from yet another perspective. He began by seeing the domestic and imperial constitutions as separate, but later went on to describe the second as something like an extension of the first. In earlier centuries, his thesis ran, England had conquered peoples—most notably, the Irish and the Welsh—who at first chafed mightily under their new rulers. Friction had eased, however, once Ireland and Wales had been brought within the English constitution—been allowed, that is, to enjoy the benefits of parliamentary institutions. The implication was that dissatisfied dependencies within the eighteenth-century empire, and Burke had America in mind, could be similarly appeased by the establishment or revitalization of government along English lines.[11] The historical accuracy of this account aside, it is not very helpful as a theoretical vision of how the empire would work. Again, however faithfully a colonial legislature might duplicate the structure and operation of the one at Westminster, the colonial body was still located on a hierarchy which found the model at the summit. To have used the Irish parliament as an analogy was particularly strange, since it is difficult to think of a legislature so impotent or with so little jurisdiction. Moreover, Burke laughed at the idea of colonial representatives actually sitting in the English Parliament, and as early as 1769 had pointed out that problems of communication over the seas would render such an arrangement no representation at all.[12] In short, Burke's idea of the imperial constitution had internal difficulties which helped undercut his practical suggestions for dealing with colonial discontent.

America

In much of the popular literature which threatened to engulf American readers during the celebration of their bicentennial anniversary as a nation, Burke was one of the few British figures treated with admiration. His voice, it was widely noted, was perhaps the most forceful in Parliament to deplore official policy. In this literature, and for generations before it in textbooks on the period, Americans have seen Burke as an heroic and sympathetic prophet of their struggle for independence. He was, of course, nothing of the sort. Rather, as his views on the empire might suggest, he was an unshakable advocate of British supremacy, but one who would have preserved it with concession rather than oppression. In 1775, he was moved to stress that America held a position of "secondary importance" within the Empire, by which he meant constitutionally secondary to the British Parliament.[13] Two years later, the best he could say for the idea of American independence was that it was a notion "to which they have been unfortunately driven. . . ."[14]

For Burke, the trouble all began in 1765 when the Grenville government secured passage of the Stamp Act. A furor immediately arose in both the colonies and British commercial circles that this means of replenishing government coffers after the costly Seven Years War was both an odious burden and a hindrance to trade. Accordingly, Rockingham's ministry repealed the tax in 1766. Had things rested there, Burke was convinced, much grief might have been avoided. As it was, the marquis's successors returned to the policy of raising revenues with colonial taxes, this time in the form of import duties sponsored in 1767 by Charles Townshend. By the end of the decade, Parliament had scrapped most of these taxes save the one on tea, left in effect to avoid the impression of utter capitulation. Again, Burke saw no reason not to restore complete harmony with an increasingly disgruntled America by abolishing *all* the new duties and returning the colonies to the *status quo ante* 1765.

It is now clear that Burke's analysis of the American question was deficient in at least two important respects. He sometimes gave the impression that he thought taxation was the only source of discord and rarely gave attention to the numerous regulations which attempted to confine the huge American overseas trade largely to Britain, and in British boats at that. Extensive smuggling subverted these regulations, which dated from the mid-seventeenth century and were known collectively as the Navigation Acts; nonetheless they were an object of angry protest in America. Yet Burke long seemed certain that the Navigation Acts could continue in full force with no adverse impact so long as Parliament would not tax the colonies. Indeed, his justification for the acts had a distinctly prescriptive ring to it: "Be content to bind America by laws of trade: you have always done it. Let this be your reason for binding their trade."[15]

Even more important, Burke was so wedded to the idea of British supremacy—even if it operated more in principle than in day-to-day practice—that he simply failed to comprehend that others might have good reasons for rejecting it. Concurrent with the repeal of the Stamp Act, the Rockingham government had also put through a Declaratory Act which reaffirmed Parliament's supreme right and power to levy taxes in the empire. In part the Declaratory Act had been designed to soothe those who disliked truckling to the impudent colonials. But in part it simply reasserted an article of faith to which Burke and all the other Rockingham Whigs—all the Members of Parliament, for that matter—were profoundly committed. It is doubtful whether Burke ever completely appreciated that the clamorous American agitation of the middle 1760s was directed as much against the principle contained in the Declaratory Act as against its fleeting application in the Stamp Act.

Essentially, then, there were three viewpoints on the American question in the early 1770s. George III and Lord North's government insisted upon asserting British authority with frequency and vigor. The Rockingham Whigs and a few other opposition splinters accepted the theory of that authority. They argued, however, that it might best be preserved by holding its direct application in abeyance for the moment and recognizing that the colonies, however subordinate in the larger scheme of things, did have certain rights.[16] But some Americans were beginning to speak a noticeably different language, in which terms like "no taxation without representation" were calling into question the whole principle of parliamentary supremacy. It was another of Burke's shortcomings that he failed to see just how serious American alienation was from a conception of the imperial constitution which he regarded as generous, liberal, and beneficial to all concerned.

By 1774, Anglo-American relations had reached crisis proportions. A Continental Congress was about to meet; there was talk of war on both sides of the Atlantic, and Lord North—fortified by a comfortable parliamentary majority—was not shrinking from it. To Burke, such talk was madness. What benefits could there possibly be in war comparable to those of a peace so easily attainable? The point of contention, as Burke saw it, was that the Parliament had altered perfectly agreeable arrangements by resorting to a new mode of taxation. In times past, he insisted, colonial legislatures had taxed themselves and thus borne their own costs of government. When special needs arose in England—when it came, for example, to financing such ventures as the Seven Years War—the colonial legislatures had made grants to the imperial Parliament in recognition that their own interests were at stake. Often, Parliament later repaid these grants. But with the Stamp Act, England asserted its new intention of unilaterally *raising* revenue from the colonies for the English treasury. Burke fully expected this scheme to produce hostility, as would most departures from long-standing ways. He begged Parliament to let the Americans tax themselves, and trust to their sense of interest and obligation to make appropriate grants in times of special necessity. "They and we, and their and our ancestors, have been happy under that system. Let the memory of all actions in contradiction to that good old mode, on both sides, be extinguished forever."[17]

Burke's favorite argument for this policy was that it had worked, and therefore would work again. He refused to justify it on "higher" grounds: "I am not here going into the distinctions of rights, nor attempting to make their boundaries. I do not enter into these metaphysical distinctions; I hate the very sound of them."[18] Here, his position was weak for being out of touch and contradictory all at once. Burke did not appreciate how pervasively the language of rights had entered into American public discussions in the preceding eight or nine years. To make matters worse, Burke was not even consistent, for he went on immediately to speak of rights himself—the "imperial rights of Great Britain." To be sure, he saw those rights as entirely reconcilable with the rights of the colonists as he conceived them. Yet the fact that he would uphold parliamentary supremacy in almost the same breath that he preached the ease of conciliation shows how remote he was from the people whose cause he thought he was supporting.

Here lies the important point about Burke's proposals for dealing with the American problem. The proper measure of their soundness was not the prevailing sense of the administration and its parliamentary majority, but rather the cutting edge of revolutionary sentiment in America. There, it had for years been accepted that the notion of parliamentary supremacy was clear-cut and admitted of either acceptance or rejection, but not modification or "interpretation." Burke's attempts to soften the implications of the doctrine, to say that while it existed in theory it need not always or even regularly materialize in practice, were virtually irrelevant in such polarized circumstances.

The effort of Burke and his party to serve as mediators was thus doubly crippled. The government had settled upon intransigence, and it had the votes. But even had Burke's program miraculously gained parliamentary support, he really had nothing to offer the

Americans that they wanted very much. They could tax themselves,
but only at the pleasure of the British Parliament. Moreover, to the
Americans it seemed that the right to legislate themselves followed
from—was indeed an inextricable part of—taxing themselves. Burke
wished not to discuss these "metaphysical distinctions," since they
would have called the whole imperial constitution into question.

As a result, Burke's justly famous speeches on the American
question, in April 1774 and March 1775, have in retrospect a
slightly futile air about them. They were noble, impassioned, models
of humanity and good sense. They disdained abstraction for a look
at specific conditions in America, and if Burke failed to see as far
as he might have, he saw farther than most of his contemporaries.
His arguments were in every sense conservative: return to past practice, to policies which worked; respect the demand for liberties
made by Americans as you respect those made by Englishmen (for
what were Americans but transplanted Englishmen?); face facts—
the Americans would not be cowed by an expensive repression any
more than they would be satisfied by indifference to their demands.
He argued the folly of attempting direct control over colonies sep-
arated by three thousand miles of ocean. His final appeal is worth
quoting at length:

All this, I know well enough, will sound wild and chimerical to the
profane herd of those vulgar and mechanical politicians who have no place
among us: a sort of people who think that nothing exists but what is gross
and material,—and who, therefore, far from being qualified to be directors
of the great movement of empire, are not fit to turn a wheel in the machine.
But to men truly initiated and rightly taught, these ruling and master
principles, which in the opinion of such men as I have mentioned have
no substantial existence, are in truth everything, and all in all. Magnanim-
ity in politics is not seldom the truest wisdom; and a great empire and
little minds go ill together. If we are conscious of our situation, and glow
with zeal to fill our place as becomes our station and ourselves, we ought
to auspicate all our public proceedings on America with the old warning
of the Church, *Sursum corda* [lift up your hearts]! We ought to elevate our
minds to the greatness of that trust to which the order of Providence has
called us. By adverting to the dignity of this high calling our ancestors
have turned a savage wilderness into a glorious empire, and have made
the most extensive and the only honorable conquests, not by destroying,
but by promoting the wealth, the number, the happiness of the human
race. . . .[19]

But it was too late, and might have been so years earlier. Before word of Burke's last speech on the subject could have reached America, the skirmishes at Lexington and Concord had taken place.

Once war had begun, Burke virtually gave up trying to shape official policy. In one last vain effort, he even proposed altering the imperial constitution by granting the American Congress not only the right to taxation but also to certain legislative powers, with the understanding that Parliament was still supreme in legislative matters. But there was no denting North's majority, and Burke's last pronouncement on the matter came in 1777. The disregard of American liberties, he was certain, could only lead to the disregard of English liberties. "By teaching us to consider our fellow citizens in an hostile light, the whole body of our nation becomes gradually less dear to us."[20] But his main impulse was not so much to try to promote a change of direction as to vent his bitterness upon those who would not change. With great feeling, he condemned the carnage and excoriated those he felt responsible for it:

. . . I cannot conceive any existence under heaven (which in the depths of its wisdom tolerates all sorts of things) that is more truly odious and disgusting than an impotent, helpless creature, without civil wisdom or military skill, without a consciousness of any other qualification for power but his servility to it, bloated with pride and arrogance, calling for battles which he is not to fight, contending for a violent domination which he can never exercise, and satisfied to be himself mean and miserable, in order to render others contemptible and wretched.[21]

Burke thus saw himself at a great distance from the managers of policy. But on the vital principle of parliamentary supremacy, it was not so great, and a year after the Declaration of Independence he implored the American rebels to be moderate and tried to convince them of the multiple advantages of continued union with the mother country.[22]

India

Burke's insistence that British dominion abroad must serve the interest of the governed was not the vacant rhetoric of a mere apologist for empire. He earnestly believed that profit alone was no excuse for the exercise of power abroad, and where he thought he saw that power wielded cruelly or capriciously at the expense of the indigenous inhabitants, he was anxious to redress the victims and punish the culpable. It was in India that he perceived the greatest abuses by British authorities, and for more than fifteen years he devoted enormous energies to correcting them.

The Indian Empire was of course vastly different from that in North America, where the governors and the governed shared the same culture. America offered expatriate Englishmen the chance to strike roots and make a new life in a congenial environment. India held out little appeal to the colonist; its attraction to the fortune-seeker, however, was magnetic. There were opportunities in trade for wealth of epic proportions, but there was also ample latitude for adventurers who knew little of commerce and, later, a huge array of lucrative and undemanding bureaucratic posts.

The East India Company was the funnel through which this manna flowed. A private corporation, chartered by the government in return for financial considerations, the Company enjoyed a commercial monopoly in India which soon brought with it extensive political functions. The native government had steadily crumbled in the first half of the eighteenth century from internal weaknesses and various local warlords sought to carve out enclaves for themselves. The East India Company and their French rivals moved in to exploit the confusion. For example, where a minor prince might be threatened by an uprising, British troops would quell it—in return for substantial payments and trading rights. When the Nawab of Bengal decided that the Company's pretensions in his sprawling territories had become intolerable, the British overthrew him, manufactured a pliable successor, accepted a generous reward for their effort, and within a short time were Bengal's virtual rulers—collecting taxes, administering justice, making all the vital decisions. Once the French had been forced out in the Seven Years War, British direct territorial holdings were relatively modest, but the Company was the decisive force on the subcontinent.

Rumors of peculation swam incessantly about the East India Company, but they do not seem to have disturbed Burke. When, in the early 1770s, Lord North's government moved to subject the Company to some greater degree of state superintendence, Burke was opposed on the ground that the "reform" was nothing less than interference with the rights of private property. Later in the decade, however, information began to come to his attention which moved him to shift his ground. As a member of a parliamentary committee empowered to investigate Indian affairs, he became convinced that certain Company officials were mired in corruption and that their treatment of the Indian population was brutal and callous. After lengthy study, he decided that the principal culprit was no less than the Governor-General of Bengal, Warren Hastings.

Not that Burke blamed imperial mismanagement entirely on one man: in 1783, he was the principal author, though not the sponsor, of a bill which would have sharply trimmed the Company's powers in India while correspondingly enlarging the overseeing powers of the state. Defending the bill in the Commons, he stated his position with startling and uncommon altruism: ". . . if we are not able to contrive some method of governing India *well*, which will not of necessity become the means of governing Great Britain *ill*, a ground is laid for their eternal separation, but none for sacrificing the people of that country to our Constitution."[23] Moreover, just as he had argued that trampling upon American rights set an unwholesome precedent for trampling upon British rights, now he maintained that the oppression of the Indians exposed the domestic constitution to "its worst corruption."[24] Again, the implication was that the domestic and imperial constitutions were nearly identical rather than separate entities, as he had first suggested in 1774.

The bills failed to pass, though largely for partisan reasons. Not long thereafter, William Pitt's newly formed administration secured acceptance of slightly refurbished versions, suggesting that on Indian as well as American matters Burke was not so far distant from his parliamentary opponents as it may have appeared. But Burke was then left with a difficult decision. He had extended himself considerably to demonstrate Hastings's personal villainy. If he let the issue drop, he could be accused of having concocted foul libels simply in order to publicize the cause of reform. But if he attempted to pursue Hastings, the prospects of success were dim and the political advantages to be gained almost nil.

Apprehensive of the result, but full of conviction that he was right, Burke pressed on, building up his case against Hastings for an eventual attempt at impeachment. Burke viewed it as a constitutional question in every respect. To begin with, colonial misrule was a malignancy at the outer limits of the constitution which always threatened, in his mind, to creep closer to the British Isles. Moreover, it was a question of upholding the law; Hastings deserved no special consideration because he was of high office and well connected:

But God forbid it should be bruited from Pekin to Paris, that the laws of England are for the rich and the powerful, but to the poor, the miserable, and the defenceless they afford no resource at all! God forbid it should be said, no nation is equal to the English in *substantial* violence and in *formal* justice,—that in this kingdom we feel ourselves competent to confer the most extravagant and inordinate powers upon public ministers, but that we are deficient, poor, helpless, lame, and impotent in the means of calling them to account for their use of them![25]

Finally, the Hastings case reinvigorated the constitution by bringing to bear the rarely employed power of impeachment, which guaranteed precisely that the rich and the powerful would have to face "competent and proportionable justice" if they transgressed in office.[26]

The impeachment process began in the House of Commons in 1786. A year later, defying all earlier predictions, Burke was able to win a favorable vote impeaching Hastings on charges ranging from several varieties of corruption to criminal provocation and exploitation of violence. In a way, the victory salvaged Burke's reputation: his colleagues had appeared to agree that his charges had substance. But this was only impeachment. The determination of innocence or guilt lay with the House of Lords, where Hastings was simply too well connected for Burke to imagine for a moment that the Commons vote would be sustained. Cruelly for Burke and Hastings alike, however, the peers sensed no particular urgency inthe case. They heard opening arguments in 1788, and they rendered the inevitable acquittal only in 1795.

In retrospect, there is nothing particularly surprising or outrageous about the acquittal. For all his labors, Burke's case was often redundant and sloppily structured, his charges sometimes carelessly drawn and questionably documented—especially when he relied heavily upon sources highly prejudiced against Hastings. Almost certainly, Hastings accumulated money in his job by unsavory means. In this, however, he was not unusual among high Company administrators in India, but merely unlucky enough to have done it when Burke was in a position to elevate the moral standards regarding high officeholders (which to some degree he almost certainly did). Besides, it could be argued with some force that Hastings was in most respects "doing his job," that is, energetically and sometimes even ruthlessly protecting and perhaps enlarging the British interest in India. That, after all, is what imperial administration has historically been about.

Yet for all the errors and excesses that Burke committed in the course of his long pursuit of Hastings, for all the occasions upon which he let temper and obstinacy overcome his best judgment, it is difficult to fault his underlying motive. He was driven from beginning to end not simply by a desire to prove his original charges, but by a tenacious attachment to the notions that misrule was unacceptable and that its perpetrators must be publicly accountable. To be satisfied with anything less was to compromise the constitution, a process which, once begun, he was certain might know no end.

Ireland

Burke's attention to Irish affairs, which spanned his entire public career, was undertaken in the tones of a sympathetic Englishman rather than in the impassioned voice of one who saw his own people wronged. This attempt to achieve some distance from his origins was politically understandable, although Burke was still unable to escape the predictable criticism that his loyalties were Irish rather than British. But the posture was more than a pose. It is hard to avoid the conclusion that Burke would have been an advocate of Irish reform no matter what the accident of his birth.

For more than thirty years, Burke hammered away at two central issues in the English governance of Ireland: religion and commerce. Not long before entering Parliament, he began an essay, the remaining fragments of which were unpublished until his death, on the extensive anti-Catholic legislation in Ireland and its grievous consequences. In his first year in the Commons, he proposed loosening the regulations which throttled Irish overseas trade and kept the island little more than a tool of English commercial interests. At least one of these two themes surfaced every time he addressed himself to Irish affairs for the rest of his life.

In the unfinished essay, Burke anticipated many of the arguments he would later make on behalf of general religious toleration. But he also saw that the Irish Catholics were in a different situation from those in England. In Ireland, the Catholics were in an overwhelming majority, so that the "Popery Laws"—which denied Catholics the right to purchase land, hold office, bear arms, or sit in the Irish Parliament, but also included insulting minor indignities such as the one which forbade them from owning a horse worth more than five pounds—were a form of discrimination directed at nearly the entire population. As such, they were manifestly improper, "for in all forms of government the people is the true legislator; and whether the immediate and instrumental cause of the law be a single person or many, the remote and efficient cause is the consent of the people, either actual or implied; and such consent is absolutely essential to its validity."[27] No one would wish to claim that the Irish people had consented to the statutes which stigmatized them because of their own religion.

Moreover, from the fact that Protestant England *legitimately* ruled Catholic Ireland, it did not follow that England *justly* ruled. Power does not automatically create authority, and Burke could think of no "error more truly subversive of all the order and beauty, of all the peace and happiness of human society" than the one which asserted that men could make whatever laws they wished simply because they were in a position to make them. A law which pretended to authority "independent of the quality of the subject matter" overlooked that there was a higher justice, "a superior law, which it is not in the power of any community, or of the whole race of man, to alter—I mean the will of Him who gave us our nature, and in giving impressed an invariable law upon it."[28]

The Popery Laws were not only unjust; they were also inefficacious. Designed allegedly to discourage—Burke thought them actually designed to punish—the practice of Catholicism, they had been singularly unsuccessful: ". . . Ireland, after almost a century of persecution, is at this hour full of penalties and full of Papists."[29] Besides, what was being persecuted? A novel and exotic sect which had but recently made its appearance? Was it not rather a venerable denomination, for centuries the established religion in Ireland? Was its tolerated practice so demonstrably destructive of social peace and order? "Society not only exists, but flourishes at this hour, with this superstition, in many countries, under every form of government,—in some established, in some tolerated, in others upon an equal footing. And was there no civil society at all in these kingdoms before the Reformation?"[30]

The Popery Laws prohibited Catholics from purchasing or inheriting most forms of property except under extremely disadvantageous conditions, and thus, Burke argued, discouraged them from improving property. So too trade regulations, which restricted Irish commerce to a few items not liable to compete with British goods, kept Ireland in a state of rustic backwardness. Although Burke claimed that a prosperous dependency was of greater benefit to England than an impoverished one, he met with stiff resistance from his Bristol merchant constituency when he supported relaxation of some of the regulations.[31] With America in revolt, and Irish nationalists mindful of the example, with Catholic France sympathetic to America and indeed to any cause likely to bring unrest in the British Empire, Burke thought it foolish not to make prudent concessions to the Irish, lest the French drift into fishing the troubled waters west of England.

In 1775, Burke had argued that the Americans could only be pacified by allowing them to enjoy their constitutional liberties, and he used the Welsh and Irish examples, among others, to support his case. "It was not English arms, but the English Constitution, that conquered Ireland."[32] This was, to say the least, stretching the facts, since Burke plainly did not believe that Ireland had much more than the trappings of constitutional government. As long as Irish Catholics could not vote, they could hardly be called citizens of their own country, much less be thought of as in any way represented by the Irish parliament.[33] Burke wanted simply to bring the constitution to life for Ireland, to make it an active and meaningful system in which Irishmen—as native-born British subjects—could participate fully. It was the same remedy he had proposed for America: let the constitution *work*, the way it had been intended to work, and most discontents would vanish.

There was, to be sure, the same qualification as in the American case: English supremacy. Burke could picture an Ireland "locally, civilly, and commercially independent" only if it looked up to "Great Britain in all matters of peace or of war,—in all those points to be guided by her,—and, in a word, with her to live and to die."[34] A completely independent Ireland was unthinkable. It would be "the most wretched, the most distracted, and, in the end, the most desolate part of the habitable globe."[35] Irish prosperity, such as it was, owed everything to its connection with England. Any attempts at defying English supremacy must be resisted. In the early 1770s, for example, the Irish parliament had proposed a tax on absentee landlords, those banes of the Irish economy who collected rents from afar while taking little cognizance of abuses committed by their local agents or of their tenants' grievances. Burke opposed the measure on several grounds, and it can hardly have been coin-

cidental that one of the larger absentee landlords who would have
been affected by the tax was the Marquis of Rockingham. One
important argument, however, was that subordinate legislatures
within the empire could not make law on imperial matters (". . . by
which I mean that law which regulates the polity and economy of
the several parts, as they relate to one another and to the whole.").
By overstepping the bounds of their proper jurisdiction, lesser legislatures threatened to "destroy the happy arrangement of the entire
empire."[36]

It was also in the English interest to retain supremacy for purely
strategic purposes. In the 1770s and the 1790s alike, Britain and
France were at war, and the French were hardly above attempting
to exploit Irish dissatisfaction. The danger grew particularly acute
in the later period, as Burke saw it, because by then the French
were not simply greedy expansionists but also fanatical revolutionaries. As will be seen later, the French Revolution gave special
urgency to Burke's pleas for reform in Ireland.[37]

A Flawed Vision

Burke knew the difference between "Hindostan" and Virginia,
and between them both and County Cork. Yet they were similar
enough in his mind that all could be encompassed within, all could
benefit richly from, the English constitution. Relativist and prag-
matist though he often was, Burke never faltered in his confidence
that the constitution could be exported to vastly different peoples
and cultures, nor did he doubt that, like a good claret, it traveled
well.

Defenders of empire do not generally make their case in terms of
sheer self-interest, of might makes right, of the inevitable triumph
and expansion of superior power. Far from presenting themselves
as in search of gain, imperialists stress what they have to offer. In
Burke's case, it was the English constitution and the immeasurable
reward of orderly liberty which was wrought into its texture. Burke
seems genuinely to have believed in the moral dimensions of the
imperial mission. He knew that "to obtain empire is common; to
govern it well has been rare indeed."[38] In his speech opening the
Hastings trial before the House of Lords, Burke expressed his vision
of that mission in terms which were undoubtedly slanted so as to
highlight the defendant's contrast to them, but which probably

come as close as anything to a distilled version of his justification for empire:

> The year 1756 is a memorable era in the history of the world: it introduced a new nation from the remotest verge of the Western world, with new manners, new customs, new institutions, new opinions, new laws, into the heart of Asia.
>
> My Lords, if, in that part of Asia whose native regular government was then broken up,—if, at the moment when it had fallen into darkness and confusion from having become the prey and almost the sport of the ambition of its home-born grandees,—if, in that gloomy season, a star had risen from the West, that would prognosticate a better generation, and would shed down the sweet influences of order, peace, science, and security to the natives of that vexed and harassed country, we should have been covered with genuine honor. It would have been a beautiful and noble spectacle to mankind.
>
> Indeed, something might have been expected of the kind, when a new dominion emanted from a learned and enlightened part of the world in the most enlightened period of its existence. Still more might it have been expected, when that dominion was found to issue from the bosom of a free country, that it would have carried with it the full benefit of the vital principle of the British liberty and Constitution, though its municipal forms were not communicable, or at least the advantage of the liberty and spirit of the British Constitution. Had this been the case, (alas! it was not,) you would have been saved the trouble of this day. It might have been expected, too, that, in that enlightened state of the world, influenced by the best religion, and from an improved description of that best religion, (I mean the Christian reformed religion,) that we should have done honor to Europe, to letters, to laws, to religion,—done honor to all the circumstances of which in this island we boast ourselves, at the great and critical moment of that revolution.[39]

There is much in this passage, of course, to offend late-twentieth-century sensibilities—the Eurocentric mentality, the unselfconscious boasting, the smug pride in superior enlightenment while Irish Catholics groaned under barbaric proscriptions and Englishmen still participated in the slave trade. Still, for their time, these are far from wholly ignoble sentiments. It is hard to believe that Burke was being hypocritical, given the circumstances of the Hastings case; these words are not a fig-leaf to mask greed, an elevated apology for plunder.

Unfortunately, at least for Indians and Irishmen, exporting the English constitution turned out to be rather more difficult than Burke imagined. Leaving aside the whole question of whether or not a society ought to be able to choose its own political system, rather than having that choice made by others, and disregarding the fact that not all Englishmen shared Burke's sense of imperial responsibility to subject peoples, it is still true that his scheme was faulty in part. The great problem was British supremacy. As long as there were areas in which the dependencies could not legislate for themselves, then colonial constitutions were a pale reflection indeed of the English model. Nor was it a small qualification that in some places the constitution's "municipal forms were not communicable." Without a solid institutional bedrock, it might prove hard to anchor the "spirit of the British constitution." On the other hand, where institutions existed which permitted some substantial degree of local participation and self-government, the whole principle of British supremacy was liable to come into question—perhaps as superfluous, ultimately as oppressive, as the Americans came to feel.

Finally, while Burke would have empire conform to principles of decency and justice, and while he would insist that it must confer benefit upon the governed in order to justify itself, the *real* empire— the one which would have existed whether Burke did or not—had an entirely independent and wholly familiar rationale. It would not have been there at all, or would have been deteriorating rapidly, had it not brought material advantage to Britain. Inescapably, that advantage would be gained at the expense of the people ruled, or, just as important, would appear to them to be gained that way. There might be very considerable by-products of value for these people. Still, if the British had not been disposed in the final analysis to rate their own interest above that of imperial subjects, there would have been no particular reason to have an empire in the first place. It was inconceivable, even if we only know this from hindsight, that British and local interests would not come into conflict from time to time, in which case decency and justice were liable to find themselves assigned a rather low priority.

The point is not that the British empire ought to have been governed according to the principles which Burke proposed. Rather, it is that no empire can be so governed. British supremacy, whether stated in constitutional terms or in terms of sheer power, was the prohibitive obstacle. In sum, Burke's view of a harmonious and beneficent diffusion of the English constitution and its libertarian traditions throughout an empire ruled by Parliament "as from the throne of heaven" was at bottom a delusion, however honorable.

Chapter Five
Society and Revolution

In 1782, Lord North's government finally came undone after a dozen years, and the Rockingham Whigs had another chance to govern. Burke neither expected nor received a ministry, although his appointment as Paymaster of the Forces was modestly lucrative. It was also brief. A few months after returning to power, the Marquis of Rockingham died, at the age of fifty-two. The government disbanded, and while Rockingham's followers returned for a while the next year in a shaky coalition, they never really had the time to shape policy decisively, although Burke was able to get through an abbreviated version of his economical reforms. A new ministry formed under the leadership of William Pitt, twenty-four years old, the second son of the Earl of Chatham, who, as William Pitt the Elder, had led the government during much of the Seven Years War. The younger Pitt was the only prime minister England would know for the rest of Burke's life.

Burke returned to opposition, then, and devoted much of his energy during the 1780s to Indian affairs and the Hastings case. Pitt brought in a walloping majority in the general election of 1784, and it seemed unlikely that he would soon be dislodged from office. The only glimmer came toward the end of 1787, when King George III mistook an oak tree for the King of Prussia and thereupon engaged it in spirited conversation. Whigs began to talk immediately of a regency in which the Prince of Wales would rule for his demented father. It made sense constitutionally, since the prince was of course the direct heir to the throne; it had a certain political appeal as well, since the heir was known to be favorable to certain Whigs. Pitt tried both to stall for time and to argue that Parliament had the right to choose whatever regent it wished. Burke objected vehemently that Pitt wanted to violate the principle of heredity upon which the constitutional succession was founded. Whether or not Burke was correct, Pitt was lucky; by the end of 1788 the king began to demonstrate increasing lucidity.

Burke turned sixty in 1789, and it is not surprising that he was having intimations of mortality. Besides Rockingham, some of his closest friends had also died—Garrick, Goldsmith, Dr. Johnson, to name the more famous. His parliamentary career had been brilliant, but largely confined to opposition; he had never attained high office, and by then knew he never would. The Hastings trial dragged on in the House of Lords, and Burke knew how it would end, though he soldiered on with it for the lack of any honorable exit. He could hardly have guessed that the work for which posterity would most highly celebrate him lay ahead.

Origins of a Masterpiece

The circumstances which prompted Burke to write the *Reflections on the Revolution in France* are well known. Charles-Jean-François Depont was a young French nobleman who knew Burke slightly and who had become marginally involved in certain early phases of the revolution. In the autumn of 1789, he wrote Burke, asking for his opinion of developments in France but really seeking some endorsement from the famous spokesman for liberty. What Depont failed to suspect was that Burke apprehended events in France in a wholly different light from the upheavals of his earlier career.

Throughout the 1770s and 1780s, Burke's pronouncements on the constitution had dealt largely with the mechanisms of government, at home and abroad. Social issues rarely surfaced in his speeches and pamphlets. But it was precisely the social dimension of the French revolution which struck him as dramatically new and of chief significance. As a consequence, his constitutional thought receives a somewhat different emphasis in the *Reflections*. It is no longer a question of maintaining a proper balance of power in institutional relationships. Rather, Burke became concerned to maintain an imbalance in social relationships which would be reflected in government.

Historically, there have been two broad interpretive approaches to the French revolution. One of them stresses political questions— a struggle for liberty, efforts to redesign government, to redistribute the powers of an absolute monarchy which had demonstrated that it could no longer manage public affairs. The other has stressed social questions—an angry revolt of the have-nots against the haves, or alternatively a "revolution of rising expectations" in which the moderately prosperous overthrow a regime which fails to satisfy their expectations of change quickly enough. In the modern Marxist variant of this latter view, an aggressive and expansive capitalist bourgeoisie displaced an effete feudal aristocracy. It was Burke, however, who gave the first thoughtful exposition to this social interpretation of the revolution.

Up to 1789, there was not much to distinguish the issues of French politics from those of the other continental states. Throughout Europe, there was conflict between centralized royal bureaucracies, which would make all politics a matter of administration, and aristocratic groups (though often with some middle-class backing) which sought a greater degree of participation in government. Indeed, the controversies over royal influence—over the "cabal," the "double cabinet," the civil list—were English versions of this same struggle. In 1788, King Louis XVI of France finally gave in to reformist pressure and convoked elections to a long-defunct representative body, the Estates-General, thus sparking hope that he would countenance proposals for change.

Had events in France continued along these lines, Burke's response would probably have been wholly different. But 1789 brought certain more threatening developments. To begin with, there was the assault upon the Bastille, when Parisian crowds in search of arms to protect themselves against a rumored punitive attack overwhelmed the old royal prison and butchered the commandant, who had formally surrendered. On the same day, the insurgents also murdered two royal officials and paraded their heads about the city on pikes. Burke took no account of the fact that a cruel economic crisis, sending up both the price of food and unemployment, had goaded the poor of the capital, or that a king who had apparently promised serious political reform had just dismissed the minister most popular among the reformers. It was the violence which startled Burke, and he expressed concern not long afterward about "the old Parisian ferocity."[1] The rising in the capital quickly spread to the countryside, where peasants in a number of regions went on a rampage against their landlords, burning aristocratic chateaux, destroying title deeds, refusing to pay taxes. Burke's apprehensions mounted, especially after he received from French friends living in the provinces a letter "which paints the miserable and precarious situation of all people of property in dreadful colours."[2]

Events continued to move quickly. The rural panic had been largely defensive, a peasant response to rumors that an angry aristocracy had employed armed hooligans to wreak punishment upon their tenants. But it had also been effective in demonstrating that the royal government could no longer maintain order. Initiative quickly passed to the National Assembly—that is, the Estates-General as rechristened by its reformist majority. The Assembly brought an end to aristocratic privilege, and thus to a number of peasant grievances. It set about drafting a constitution for France which would limit the powers of the monarchy and enhance those of the legislature, which had not even met during the previous century and a half. It laid down the principles for that constitution in a Declaration of the Rights of Man and the Citizen late that summer. It also found that the king was taking every opportunity not to cooperate with its work. In early October, therefore, certain impatient members of the National Assembly succeeded in channeling popular economic grievances among the Paris poor against the monarchy. A large crowd marched on the suburban royal palace at Versailles and forced the royal family to return to a residence in Paris itself—where the king might be more easily intimidated by the presence of the mob.

Finally, the Assembly continued to face serious difficulties in public finance. The near bankruptcy of the government, which had brought Louis XVI to his knees and forced him to call the long-dormant legislature, was probably as important a precipitating cause of the revolution as any. But the fall of the Bastille did not reduce the debt. Finally, the Assembly hit upon a solution which appeared to solve two problems at once. For years, reformers and social critics had made a special target of the Catholic Church for what they deemed its obscurantism, its stranglehold on education, its participation in the odious system of censorship, its exploitation of the peasant tenantry on its extensive landholdings, its refusal—like the aristocracy—to pay taxes on its wealth, and its general tendency to join the ranks of those who resisted change. Briefly put, the Assembly decided to bring the Church under the direct control of the state—clergy became civil servants, paid (as in England) from public funds—and to put Church property "at the disposal of the nation." Church lands were nationalized, then put up for sale to the public.

When Burke heard of these measures, which he referred to as "pil-lage," he drew the line and pronounced France "a country undone; and irretrievable for a very long Course of time."[3] At about the same time, he received the inquiry from Depont.

The ruin of a major country was no small affair; Burke found the revolution "the most astonishing that has hitherto happened in the world."[4] Understandably, however, he was concerned first of all for the safety of England, and there were unmistakable danger signs at home. Too few people seemed to grasp the ominous implications of events in France. Some of his own Whig colleagues were favorably disposed toward developments across the Channel. Meanwhile, the "democratic" reformers were putting it about that the French rev-olution was entirely consistent with, was indeed a new application of, the principles of England's revolution of 1688. Burke found this sort of thinking lunacy. From the radicals, of course, such as the dissenting preacher Dr. Richard Price, one could expect no better, but Burke bemoaned the shortsightedness of men who, he thought, would have known better. In February 1790, he attempted to con-front the Commons with what he took for the reality of the revolution:

He wished the House to consider how the members would like to have their mansions pulled down and pillaged, their persons abused, insulted, and destroyed, their title-deeds brought and burned before their faces, and themselves and their families driven to seek refuge in every nation throughout Europe, for no other reason than this, that, without any fault of theirs, they were born gentlemen and men of property, and were sus-pected of a desire to preserve their consideration and their estates.[5]

It was in this temper that Burke continued to expand his answer to Depont. It finally appeared in print, on 1 November 1790.

Men of No Property

The most difficult task for a reader of the *Reflections* is to keep from being simply overwhelmed by the book. For it is a deeply passionate statement, one felt as much as thought, and Burke ex-pressed his feelings in extraordinarily compelling language. The organization contributes to the same end. Burke retained the episto-lary format of his first response to Depont, which permitted him a somewhat more personal, even intimate, tone and a commanding use of direct address which turns the reader into a riveted "you."[6]

There are no chapters, no subheadings to divide the whole; Burke keeps coming at the reader, indefatigably, for something better than 90,000 words. There is also about the *Reflections* something of the awesome quality of a *summa*. In a sense, everything that Burke believed about man, society, and politics is in this work, and thus it is very far from being merely a set of "reflections" on events in France. It is a sweeping and powerful defense of an entire way of life, a furious rejection of principles and behavior which Burke regarded as a direct threat to civilization itself.

It is impossible, at least in the space allotted here, to undertake an analysis of the *Reflections* by beginning with the first paragraph and proceeding directly through to the last. Burke worked on too many levels at nearly the same time, veered too often back and forth from France to England, moved too easily from description to philosophical statement, to make such an expository procedure useful. The reading of the *Reflections* offered here draws therefore upon recurrent themes and arguments throughout the book and attempts to put them together in a way which represents, if it does not exactly resemble, the whole.

On the numerous occasions earlier in his career when Burke had defended and commended his political party, he had frequently included among the attributes of the Rockingham Whigs the fact that they were men of property. It was not until 1790, however, that Burke revealed how much importance he attached to that fact. When Burke complained, "The property of France does not govern it," he was making no minor criticism.[7]

He insisted that he intended no simple identification of the right to rule with noble title. "There is no qualification for government, but virtue and wisdom, actual or presumptive."[8] A good deal of his political thinking is contained within this sentence, although Burke himself does not much elaborate on it. What he seems to have meant was that "actual" virtue and wisdom would show themselves unmistakably, would be so apparent to any thoughtful observer as to obviate the need for quibbling about them. "Actual" virtue and wisdom would prove themselves in practice. But on what grounds would one "presume" virtue and wisdom of a person (the implication being that the "presumptive" varieties would be less immediately self-evident than the "actual")? Why would one think of a person that he had a "qualification for government" before he had demonstrated it beyond doubt?

The questions are best answered by keeping in mind what Burke thought about politics. Public service was a demanding and complicated task involving attention to the most extensive detail and an ability to summon a general overview at the same time. It took an appreciation of varying and sometimes conflicting interests; it demanded skill and subtlety in organizing compromises, the very stuff of politics; it called for the independence to be able to stand up to power, whether that of an overweening court or of a narrow-minded constituency. Where, within the social order, would one be most likely to find people one could presume to be equal to those tasks? Burke quoted from Ecclesiastes: "The wisdom of a learned man cometh by opportunity of leisure; and he that hath little business shall become wise.—How can he get wisdom that holdeth the plough, and that glorieth in the goad; that driveth oxen, and is occupied in their labours; and whose talk is of bullocks?" While it was conceivable that "actual" virtue and wisdom might be found throughout the social hierarchy, though not necessarily in equally distributed proportions, its appearance was rare enough. "Presumptive" virtue and wisdom were to be found among the propertied elements, and the more property a man owned, the more virtue and wisdom one could presume because of the leisure, the education, the refinement one could observe. Moreover, there was an historical dimension to consider. The owners of substantial property always had ruled, and therefore were educated to their responsibilities from youth, brought up in surroundings where the experience of governance was prominent. Plainly, then, one had more reason to presume their qualification to rule than any other social order. Thus, for one example, while Burke would not say that titled nobility per se qualified one to govern, the persons whom he presumed qualified to govern were nearly always—because of their wealth—members of the nobility.

Yet there was another reason why the responsibilities of government ought to rest with large property-holders, and that was to protect property itself. The terms in which Burke put this argument were philosophically clumsy, but essentially he was saying that rich people ought to have power so that they could protect their wealth from the envy of the poor. In the process, however, they would also protect lesser forms of property, and thus benefit society at large.

All these views point to an underlying motif which was not in the least bit novel but nonetheless of the greatest importance. Private property was unevenly distributed—Burke would not have been embarrassed to say radically so—and it was in the nature of things that it remain that way. Social inequality was an inescapable fact of life, an historical constant from which, it so happened, considerable benefits flowed. For one thing, great proprietors would be especially sensitive to the rights of all property in order to fortify their own rights, and the right to private property, as we shall see, was closely bound to liberty itself. For another, it was the great concentrations of wealth which provided the patronage for learning and art, and thus elevated life above mere survival.

Rarely before had Burke found it necessary to argue that the social hierarchy implied and even created a political hierarchy; the subject had rarely come up, the connection had been widely taken for granted. The French revolutionaries, however, and their admirers in England, were now talking an entirely different political language—that of natural rights, or what Burke liked to stigmatize as "the rights of men." In this view, a man's natural rights were those he possessed by virtue not of his wealth, or social eminence, or education, or refinement, or political experience, or ability, but rather by his nature—by the fact that he was a human being. Burke considered such notions "metaphysical," and therefore dangerous, especially if the statement of such rights included the right to govern. *Who* governed was not a matter of rights, but a matter of what he called "convention," a question to be settled according to the dictates of public "convenience" or utility. It most certainly could not be settled in the abstract realm, where so much preposterous reasoning took place because of a failure to consider circumstances. "Is it because liberty in the abstract may be classed amongst the blessings of mankind, that I am seriously to felicitate a madman, who has escaped from the protecting restraint and wholesome darkness of his cell, on his restoration to the enjoyment of light and liberty?"[9]

Men did have rights, but they existed only in a circumstantial context—civil society, where the rule of convention tempered so much. Men created civil society in order to enjoy certain benefits; therefore, argued Burke, they have a right to those benefits—for example, living under the rule of law, and receiving justice from it; receiving the fruits of their own labor, and inheriting those of their parents; doing whatever they wish for themselves so long as they do not inhibit other men in the exercise of *their* rights. For all this, however, it was still true that "all men have equal rights, but not to equal things."[10] Men had equal rights to property—a peasant owned his tiny plot as surely as a baron owned his huge estate—but not rights to equal property.

Moreover, "the management of the state" was not a right; if it had ever existed, the very creation of civil society canceled it out. In the "state of nature"—a concept Burke used only as an analytical device—men might legitimately lay claim to a broad array of rights, but there was no power which could guarantee that they could enjoy them. Man's assertion of his liberty constantly ran up against similar assertions from his neighbors. In order to adjudicate such disputes, man created the state, but in the process, as Burke put it, "That he may secure some liberty, he makes a surrender in trust of the whole of it."[11] He created a sovereign authority which then decides, according to the dictates of public utility, how much liberty will be returned to him. The amount would vary from time to time and place to place: "It is a thing to be settled by convention."[12]

There was no universal formula for the amount of liberty men might enjoy, save one: it could never be total. For human nature itself was such that "perfect liberty" meant nothing short of chaos. In a famous passage, Burke turned the language of rights back upon his opponents:

Government is a contrivance of human wisdom to provide for human *wants*. Men have a right that these wants should be provided for by this wisdom. Among these wants is to be reckoned the want, out of civil society, of a sufficient restraint upon their passions. Society requires not only that the passions of individuals should be subjected, but that even in the mass and body as well as in the individuals, the inclinations of men should frequently be thwarted, their will controlled, and their passions brought into subjection.[13]

Interestingly enough, thirteen years earlier Burke had started from the same contempt for abstractions in a discussion of American affairs but had moved toward rather different conclusions:

The *extreme* of liberty (which is its abstract perfection, but its real fault) obtains nowhere, nor ought to obtain anywhere; because extremes, as we all know, in every point which relates either to our duties or satisfactions in life, are destructive both to virtue and enjoyment. Liberty, too, must be limited in order to be possessed. The degree of restraint it is impossible in any case to settle precisely. But it ought to be the constant aim of every wise public counsel to find out by cautious experiments, and rational, cool endeavors, with how little, not how much, of this restraint the community can subsist: for liberty is a good to be improved, and not an evil to be lessened. It is not only a private blessing of the first order, but the vital spring and energy of the state itself, which has just so much life and vigor as there is liberty in it. [14]

The revolution forced Burke to change his emphasis; his concern now was with subjecting, thwarting, controlling. It would be absurd to have government in the grip of precisely those passions which government had been designed to subject in the first place. Of course, there is always the question of who subjects the subjectors, though for Burke it was apparently a negligible one, largely solved by the presumably superior virtue of the governors and by the fact that—in England, at least—the constitution was spread through three institutions which might check one another.

If it were possible to govern according to the abstract and universal dictates of natural rights, then of course nothing would be simpler. But when one had to be sensitive to both public "convenience" and the peculiarities of human nature, governance became an awesomely complicated task.

The nature of man is intricate; the objects of society are of the greatest possible complexity; and therefore no simple disposition or direction of power can be suitable either to man's nature, or to the quality of his affairs. When I hear the simplicity of contrivance aimed at and boasted of in any new political constitutions, I am at no loss to decide that the artificers are grossly ignorant of their trade, or totally negligent of their duty. The simple governments are fundamentally defective to say no worse of them. [15]

Consequently, government had no business in the hands of the uneducated, the inexperienced, the simple-minded, the short-sighted, who would mismanage and in the end destroy it—not to mention the base and the greedy, who would loot it as well.

The problem in France was thus easily defined. The wrong sort of people governed the country, people who only compounded the difficulty by holding the wrong sort of ideas. "Rights of men" or no "rights of men," the social station of most members of the National Assembly brought France to ruin. It was what Burke called "the cause of all," and he claimed, "From the moment I read the list [of members] I saw distinctly, and very nearly as it has happened, all that was to follow."[16]

Who were these legislators? Once a number of horrified aristocrats and higher clergy had withdrawn from the Assembly, and some of them from the country, representatives of the commons predominated. Of these, lawyers made up the largest contingent—but not, Burke was quick to note, judges, renowned advocates, or learned professors. Mostly, he found small-town attorneys and petty notaries, men of little standing in their profession who could therefore hardly be expected to summon much self-respect. Having no practical understanding of the state, they would simply continue to pursue their private interests. (Burke failed to note that a large proportion of the Assembly's lawyers had served in government, and might lay claim to some knowledge of its workings.) As they had made their livings by litigation—the more, the better for them thought Burke—then they would produce a *"litigious constitution."* "Was it to be expected that they would attend to the stability of property, whose existence had always depended upon whatever rendered property questionable, ambiguous, and insecure?"[17]

Alongside them stood a motley collection of obscure physicians, financial speculators, "who must be eager, at any expence, to change their ideal paper wealth for the more solid substance of land," and a large representation from the lower clergy. This last group gave Burke special concern. Their horizons had never extended beyond the village boundaries, they "never had seen the state so much as in a picture," were hopelessly impoverished and therefore bound to be a threat to the property of others.[18] Finally, there were a few adventurers and discontents from the nobility, traitors to their order, allies in the ugly conspiracy to despoil it.

For such was surely the chief design of the National Assembly: the destruction of the nobility in the interests of social equality and the redistribution of property. Once begun, however, leveling was not easily arrested. What was left of the present generation of nobility would soon disappear.

The next generation of the nobility will resemble the artificers and clowns, and money-jobbers, usurers, and Jews, who will be always their fellows, sometimes their masters. Believe me, Sir, those who attempt to level, never equalize. In all societies, consisting of various descriptions of citizens, some description must be uppermost. The levellers therefore only change and pervert the natural order of things; they load the edifice of society, be setting up in the air what the solidity of the structure requires to be on the ground. [19]

Burke would have taken no consolation from the knowledge that the National Assembly insisted upon a property qualification for the franchise in its new constitution. Once the Assembly had disrupted the "natural" order of society by hurling the nobility from the apex, then the worst was bound to come soon: "The occupation of an hair-dresser, or of a working tallow-chandler, cannot be a matter of honour to any person—to say nothing of a number of other more servile employments. Such descriptions of men ought not to suffer oppression from the state; but the state suffers oppression, if such as they, either individually or collectively, are permitted to rule. In this you think you are combatting prejudice, but you are at war with nature." [20]

Burke was at pains to defend not only a traditional social structure but what he took to be a code of behavior as well. In a long and remarkable passage, he described the so-called October Days when a Paris crowd marched on Versailles and brought the royal family back to the capital in its train. Burke expressed shock and horror at this disgusting and degrading treatment of royalty. (He also let his imagination run free briefly and recounted an attempt upon the queen's life which never took place.) In language which embarrassed even some of his supporters, Burke compared Marie Antoinette's present situation with his recollection of her on a trip to France in 1773:

It is now sixteen or seventeen years since I saw the queen of France, then the dauphiness, at Versailles; and surely never lighted on this orb, which she hardly seemed to touch, a more delightful vision. I saw her just about the horizon, decorating and cheering the elevated sphere she just began to move in,—glittering like the morning-star, full of life, and splendor, and joy. Oh! what a revolution! and what an heart must I have, to contemplate without emotion that elevation and that fall. [21]

How had she come to the debasement of the October Days? "I thought ten thousand swords must have leaped from their scabbards to avenge a look that threatened her with insult." [22] But something had changed: a loutish mob could invade the royal bedchamber because the values which once would have stirred those swords no longer existed. In Burke's own words, "the age of chivalry is gone."[23]

Burke's nostalgia can be difficult for the twentieth-century mind to comprehend. In our time, the notion of chivalry prompts images of a stiff and hollow etiquette, of bold knights thrashing dragons on behalf of menaced damsels. Burke had something else in mind. He saw the chivalric spirit as one which infused ordinary social relationships with a sense of dignity and honor, which elevated the upper levels of the hierarchy with "that generous loyalty to rank and sex, that dignified obedience, that subordination of the heart, which kept alive, even in servitude itself, the spirit of an exalted freedom."[24]

The elaborate etiquette, particularly that which surrounded the court, may have been artificial, but these were "pleasing illusions, which made power gentle, and obedience liberal. . . ." Chivalry was a "decent drapery" cast over the harsh realities of life, a cloak of gentle and gratifying manners which tried to make the world more beautiful. In its absence, worldly ugliness asserted itself monstrously: ". . . a king is but a man; a queen is but a woman; a woman is but an animal; and an animal not of the highest order. All homage paid to the sex in general as such, and without distinct views, is to be regarded as romance and folly."[25] Modern rationalist philosophy, which had given us the "rights of men," would deprive the world of all its elegance. "Nothing is left which engages the affections on the part of the commonwealth." There was no longer fealty to a king, veneration for a queen; the aesthetic response had been drained out of political life. Laws would be obeyed out of terror, out of fear for punishment. It was good that laws were obeyed, but not like that. Without an attractive system of manners and mores, without affection or admiration for social and political institutions, without a special mystique to enfold royalty, or aristocracy, or clergy, society became desiccated and mechanistic. "To make us love our country, our country ought to be lovely."[26]

Burke knew that this section of the *Reflections* would subject him to ridicule. After all, if the age of chivalry were truly gone, how many survivors were around to appreciate the loss? Earlier in 1790, a friend familiar with the progress of the manuscript had found the prose on Marie Antoinette a bit moist, and said so. Burke responded:

I tell you again that the recollection of the manner in which I saw the Queen of France . . . and the contrast between that brilliancy, Splendour, and beauty, with the prostrate Homage of a Nation to her, compared with the abominable Scene of 1789 which I was describing did draw Tears from me and wetted my Paper. These Tears came again into my Eyes almost as often as I looked at the description. They may again. You do not believe this fact, or that these are my real feelings, but that the whole is affected, or as you express it, "downright Foppery." My friend, I tell you it is truth—and that it is true, and will be true, when you and I are no more, and will exist as long as men—with their Natural feelings exist.[27]

The same defense found its way into the *Reflections*. Chivalry may have been a sort of social aesthetics, a "pleasing illusion," but if it was artificial, the response it evoked was not. To the contrary, it was an entirely authentic expression of human nature when "our passions instruct our reason."[28]

People in England found nothing strange in this, thought Burke, because the French disease—in this case, rationalist philosophy— had not yet infected them. The intellectual arrogance which led the French *philosophes* to place so much confidence in human reason remained foreign; Englishmen understood their own intellectual limitations, trusted their "inbred sentiments" to guide them as they always had. "We preserve the whole of our feelings still native and entire, unsophisticated by pedantry and infidelity. We have real hearts of flesh and blood beating in our bosoms. We fear God; we look up with awe to kings; with affection to parliaments; with duty to magistrates; with reverence to priests; and with respect to no- bility. Why? Because when such ideas are brought before our minds, it is *natural* to be so affected. . . ."[29] The English mind, Burke boasted, far from drawing upon some sterile and suspiciously novel philosophy for guidance, took much pride in its preference for lean- ing on prejudice.

Again, it is a word that jars. The twentieth century has made efforts, however feeble, to overcome rather than to take pride in its prejudices. Yet no one familiar with Burke's stand on religious toleration can suppose him to have encouraged bigotry. What he meant in the *Reflections* was the same thing he had meant in the *Vindication of Natural Society:* certain things ought to be beyond speculation and analysis. On certain questions—listed in the quo- tation above—it was better that people *pre*-judged, that they ac-

cepted certain institutions and practices because their responses to
them "felt right." It would be as chaotic for each generation to
resubmit all their values to intellectual scrutiny as it would for each
generation to wipe clean the slate upon which the constitution was
written and begin writing anew. Prejudice respected history, and
it anchored respect far more firmly than ratiocination because it was
rooted in feeling.

You see, Sir, that in this enlightened age I am bold enough to confess,
that we are generally men of untaught feelings; that instead of casting
away all our old prejudices, we cherish them to a very considerable degree,
and, to take more shame to ourselves, we cherish them because they are
prejudices; and the longer they have lasted, and the more generally they
have prevailed, the more we cherish them. We are afraid to put men to
live and trade each on his own private stock of reason; because we suspect
that this stock in each man is small, and that the individuals would do
better to avail themselves of the general bank and capital of nations, and
ages.[30]

The wrong men and the wrong principles had brought social
revolution. Defiance of the social and political hierarchies and a
witless commitment to the "rights of men" had put France on a
road known by men of good sense to be the way to anarchy and
oblivion. This is what had happened in France. But why had it
happened? Again, Burke resorted to a social interpretation.

Men of Ill Property

In the National Assembly, the lawyers had figured prominently.
As Burke looked at prerevolutionary France, however, his eye fell
rather upon financiers, speculators, *rentiers,* urban bourgeoisie whom
Burke grouped together as the "monied interest." Quite at variance
with present-day scholarship, he saw a great cleavage between this
group and the "landed interest" dominated by the nobility; recent
research has revealed that each sector of the economy invested substantially in the other.[31] In any event, before the haughtiness of
noble title, the monied interest often felt "an inferiority, the grounds
of which they did not acknowledge."[32] They sought revenge for
their treatment and a higher estimation for their impressively expanding wealth.

In Burke's not very convincing account, the monied interest determined upon an indirect attack on the nobility through the prop-

erty of the church, every last one of whose bishops was also a noble by the 1780s. But they did not attempt the attack alone. They were aided by the "political Men of Letters"—the *philosophes* of the French Enlightenment—who undertook a campaign to discredit the clergy, undermine the church, and destroy Christianity. At the same time, they used their literary skills to give the monied interest a better press while extending their vicious satires from the clergy to the nobility and the court. The revolution was the first fruit of this campaign, the confiscation of church property the second.

Burke was not in the slightest prepared to accept the notion that the French government's financial situation was in fact calamitous. He had long been impressed by the published review of the treasury in 1780 by Jacques Necker, the Minister of Finance. Burke never understood that Necker had doctored up his account in order to embellish his own reputation. Burke saw the French nation as flush and opulent in resources. If the monarchy was a little short on cash, let it impose a new tax. Of course, the whole point of convoking the Estates-General had been that public confidence in the crown had so plummeted that a new tax without some reformist concessions would have touched off serious civil disorders. Government indebtedness was real and huge; bondholders wanted their interest, lenders their principal. Burke regarded their demands with contempt: "Upon any insolvency they ought to suffer who were weak enough to lend upon bad security. . . ."[33] The rights of property, it would appear, did not have to be universally secure.

The seizure of church property was more than a violation of a basic right which established a sad precedent for other forms of property. It was also the violation of a basic institution. Deprive a gentleman of his property, and you deprived him of his independence. It was the same with the church. Clerics were obliged to mix in society, where the general view of poverty was one of disapproval. "Our provident constitution has therefore taken care that those who are to instruct presumptuous ignorance, those who are to be censors over insolent vice, should neither incur their contempt, nor live upon their alms. . . ."[34] But there was more to it than simply a question of social *cachet*. According to Burke, the English people

do not consider their church establishment as convenient, but as essential to their state; not as a thing heterogeneous and separable; something added for accommodation; what they may either keep up or lay aside, according to their temporary ideas of convenience. They consider it as the foundation of their whole constitution, with which, and with every part of which, it holds an indissoluble union. Church and state are ideas inseparable in their minds, and scarcely is the one ever mentioned without mentioning the other.[35]

To strip the church of its properties was to attack government itself. It was to undermine the institution which infused the state with eternal values and consecrated it in the eyes of its citizens, generated in them "an wholesome awe," and connected the governors with the "one great master, author and founder of society."[36]

The nationalization of church land, then, was bad enough, and not far from sacrilege; but the worst was yet to come. The subsequent sale of church lands brought with it an evil of incalculable malignancy—the *assignats,* bonds secured by the land itself which could be used for its purchase, but which soon began to function as something close to currency. Burke was something less than fond of the innovation: "So violent an outrage upon credit, property, and liberty, as this compulsory paper currency, has seldom been exhibited by the alliance of bankruptcy and tyranny, at any time, or in any nation."[37] Worse, the *assignats'* effect was that they permitted and even promoted a brisk trade in landed property. Now property, thought Burke, was by nature "sluggish, inert, and timid"—or, to put it more positively, stable.[38] Once this vigorous trade in land is under way, "the spirit of money-jobbing and speculation goes into the mass of land itself, and incorporates with it. By this kind of operation, that species of property becomes, as it were, volatilized" and thus acquires "the worst and most pernicious part of the evil of a paper circulation, the greatest possible uncertainty in its value."[39]

Once uncertainty sets in, can social collapse be far behind? Burke proceeded to sketch out two visions of the chaos which must follow from this infection of the society by "the spirit of money-jobbing and speculation." The first was economic. Values will fluctuate wildly; therefore, "Industry must wither away. Economy must be driven from your country. Careful provision will have no existence. Who will labor without knowing the amount of his pay? Who will study to increase what none can estimate? Who will accumulate, when he does not know the value of what he saves?"[40] The second was social. When the peasant sells his produce in the market, he is forced to take the mercurial *assignat* at par. This would be fair enough, except that he quickly discovers that in a shop on the same street the wretched bill is "seven per cent the worse for crossing the way." Peasants will be henceforth reluctant to produce for the town market, and the townsmen will in turn force them to bring in food. The peasants will resist, and bloodshed is inevitable.

In the struggle between two sharply opposed forms of property which Burke saw in France's future, each form was identified with a distinct physical location, and Burke was convinced the advantage must always go to the urban monied interest. Far from supposing that rural society was in some sense organically bonded together, Burke at this juncture described it as wholly atomized, incapable of implementing anything "in the nature of incorporation." Overlooking the behavior of French peasants during the summer of 1789, he insisted that men of the countryside "assemble, they arm, they act, with the utmost difficulty, and at the greatest charge. Their efforts, if ever they can be commenced, cannot be sustained. They cannot proceed systematically." For townspeople, on the other hand, "combination is natural. The habits of burghers, their occupations, their diversion, their business, their idleness, continually bring them into mutual contact."[41]

The victory of the urban monied interest would not halt the unraveling of the French social fabric. As Burke put it a few years later, the "contempt of Property . . . that has led to all the other evils which have ruined France" would ultimately endanger *all* property.[42] The whole social pyramid would tremble if one tampered with its pinnacle. Having been corrupted into performing as the revolutionary shock troops by "the Spoil of the superiour Classes," the "low and feeble" would not long sit still for what amounted to a petty bribe. The peasants, instructed by the men of letters that all things "feudal" were bad, could well insist that the land revert to them as the descendants of the prefeudal Gauls. Or, they might claim that equal shares of the earth were due them by the "rights of men." Then again, they might argue that "the occupant and subduer of the soil is the true proprietor . . . ."[43] The monied interest's enjoyment of clerical and noble lands would be brief. As Burke later put it with a certain pungency, "If the formation of a government was committed to the no-property people, the first thing they would do, obviously would be to plunder those who had property, and the next thing would be to plunder and massacre each other."[44]

In sum, what had begun with the church could not stop with the church. Looking back from 1793, Burke ticked off the list: after the church came the confiscation of the royal domain, then the properties of the king's brothers, to be followed swiftly by that of the nobility. "At length the monied and the moveable property tumbled on the ruin of the immoveable property—and at this day, no Magazine, from the Warehouses of the East India company to the Grovers and the Bakers shop, possesses the smallest degree of safety."[45] It is significant in this eighteenth-century version of the domino theory that the monied interest itself was soon overwhelmed as thoroughly as the landed interest, so that France ended up "directed by *the refuse of its chicane.*"[46]

Needless to say, Burke's concern for the fate of French property was really concern for the future of English property.[47] Having heaped scorn upon the idea that the French government's debt had justified confiscation, he suddenly conceived of circumstances in which the English government's debt might reach proportions where an "extensive discontented monied interest" would attempt to follow the example of their European counterparts. In order to avoid the attendant catastrophe, it was imperative that the English remain tenacious in their commitment to the rights of ownership.

There appears to be no way to overstate the importance which the security of private property had come to assume in Burke's thought. In 1794, he spoke to the House of Commons about the future restoration of order in France once the revolution had been destroyed:

> It was not for any particular system of government that he contended, but for some government. Let it be a pure monarchy, a democracy, or an aristocracy, or all mixed, he cared not, provided a government did exist, the first principle of which must necessarily be security to property, because, for the protection of property, all governments were instituted. First, therefore, restore property, and afterwards let that property find a government for itself.
>
> ....
>
> After all, if it were asked, did he prefer property to virtue? his answer would be no. To honour?—No. To morals?—No. To arts and literature?—No. But he respected property in as much as it was the basis upon

which they were all erected—the soul that animated, the genius that protected them.[48]

Property, or at least large concentrations of it, had long been the "soul that animated" European arts and literature. The Roman Catholic church had been the repository and guardian of culture for centuries. Aristocratic patronage had provided critical stimulus and support. Thus it was particularly painful for Burke to see French intellectuals turn on the clergy and the nobility—for centuries their natural allies—and align themselves with a revolutionary populace which must inevitably overwhelm them and destroy all that they ought to have stood for. "Happy if learning, not debauched by ambition, had been satisfied to continue the instructor, and not aspired to be the master! Along with its natural protectors and guardians, learning will be cast into the mire, and trodden down under the hoofs of a swinish multitude."[49]

The security of property in something like its present distribution in England was also vital to the operation of the economic system. The evident disparities were actually functional. Take all the property in England, divide it up among the population by equal shares, and what would you have? Each person would own a pitifully small piece. The great accumulations could perform economic services which the tiny fragments could not. Large landlords were also large consumers of both goods and labor.[50] Poorer people could simply not afford for the richer to stop buying and stop employing. Moreover, where property was secure, a society could expect the advantages correspondent to the disadvantages Burke predicted in a France tyrannized by the *assignat*. Where one could count on owning tomorrow what one owned today, there would be industriousness, frugality, investment—in a word, prosperity.

Government ought to do everything in its power to protect property rights, but it ought to do very little else regarding property lest it impede the "natural" workings of economic forces. There is no economic theory in the *Reflections,* only a series of scattered hints, but they all point in the same direction. Burke was a friend of Adam Smith's, and he subscribed to the general principles of *The Wealth of Nations.* From Burke's writings and speeches it is possible to glean numerous familiar maxims of the so-called laissez-faire school, often stated with the fervor of a Dickensian parody:

I would have the people of this island know, that if they would be relieved, they must relieve themselves by an increase of industry. There is no other possible remedy. People may talk of charity and parliamentary aid, but I am afraid these will in the end prove ineffectual. If the people of England should take it in their heads to idle away one day extraordinary, no human contrivance could indemnify them.[51]

If it were not generally pernicious to disturb the natural course of things, and to impede, in any degree, the great wheel of circulation. . . .[52]

. . . you had all that combination, and all that opposition of interests, you had that action and counteraction which, in the natural and in the political world, from the reciprocal struggle of discordant powers, draws out the harmony of the universe.[53]

Labor is a commodity like every other, and rises or falls according to the demand. This is in the nature of things; however, the nature of things has provided for their necessities.[54]

We, the people, ought to be made sensible that it is not in breaking the laws of commerce, which are the laws of God, that we are to place our hope of softening the Divine displeasure to remove any calamity under which we suffer or which hangs over us.[55]

When it came to property, government's role was to secure, not to interfere. Occasionally, this meant resigning oneself to some strange circumstances. Property-owners might exploit their tenants, or on the other hand fail to exploit their property to its capacities. They might use their profits for wasteful purchases. Still, in order to protect the rights to property more beneficially employed, one had to protect the rights to all property. And in any case, the profits would diffuse themselves. If the monks of France chose to use the income from their holdings to build a monument to some saint, the workmen they employed were at least employed—and no more uselessly than if their sweat flowed for the construction of a brothel. There was no alternative to "the necessity of submitting to the yoke of luxury and the despotism of fancy, who in their own imperious way will distribute the surplus product of the soil. . . ."[56]

The distribution of that product would be unequal. Moreover, in order that the whole system could function, some persons were unavoidably condemned to "the innumerable servile, degrading, unseemly, unmanly, and often most unwholesome and pestiferous occupations, to which by the social economy so many wretches are inevitably doomed."[57] Burke seems genuinely to have felt for such people, but there was nothing to be done for them. Government could not maintain the poor; rather, the poor maintained the rich by being numerous and thus holding down wages while having little choice but to perform those "pestiferous occupations."[58]

If government showed any signs of exceeding its appropriate authority on questions of property, Burke was usually on his feet. The idea of a property reevaluation for tax purposes made him nervous.[59] He characterized the unwarranted taxation of America as "AN ATTEMPT MADE TO DISPOSE OF THE PROPERTY OF A WHOLE PEOPLE WITHOUT THEIR CONSENT."[60] During the American war, British troops invaded the Dutch possession of St. Eustatius in the West Indies and confiscated private property belonging to both Dutch and British subjects. Although Burke was unable to repay the damage, still he lectured the House of Commons at length, eventually working himself into such a lather that he could discuss the question of "dethroning" kings:

. . . in all government there is a trust reposed. "Show me a government," said Mr. Burke, "and I will show a trust"; and a king must abandon that trust, he must give up his royalty and his government, when he seizes upon the property of the subject; he must dethrone himself from the just dominion when he becomes the unjust plunderer of his people; and when he thus departs from the character and the dignity and the office of a king, to take up that of a robber and a spoiler, there is a sword in every hand to execute upon him the vengeance of human nature.[61]

In his own plan for economical reform, Burke was scrupulous to exempt from the general housecleaning certain patent offices in the Exchequer for the reason that they "have been considered as property."[62]

At one point in the *Reflections,* Burke conceded that wealth will often indulge itself in "fopperies and follies." But, he argued, "We tolerate them, because property and liberty, to a degree, require that toleration."[63] The linkage between these two concepts was no accident; indeed, Burke thought it indissoluble. Liberty included the liberty to dispose of one's property as one saw fit; the mode of usage had no bearing upon title to it. Moreover, property provided liberty. It gave a man independence, buffered him against a potentially intrusive government, and on a social scale the great properties protected the smaller.

Since liberty did not arise from the "rights of men," where did it come from? The liberties of Englishmen, at least, had the same source as their property: they were inherited. Burke took it to be "the uniform policy of our constitution to claim and assert our liberties, as an *entailed inheritance* derived to us from our forefathers, and to be transmitted to our posterity . . ." As monarchs inherited the crown, as the peers inherited their titles, so the House of Commons and the people inherited "privileges, franchises, and liberties, from a long line of ancestors."[64] The system made for security, but its highest virtue was that it conformed to a larger and "higher" process of nature: "By a constitutional policy, working after the pattern of nature, we receive, we hold, we transmit our government and our privileges, in the same manner in which we enjoy and transmit our property and our lives. The institutions of policy, the goods of fortune, the gifts of Providence, are handed down, to us and from us, in the same course and order. Our political system is placed in a just correspondence and symmetry with the order of the world. . . ."[65] As life itself was a gift from an earlier generation, so too with property and with the state. Thus the English social and political systems were unified not only with one another, but with the principles by which God had decreed the world would operate.

Such a vision both reflected and demanded respect for the past. Burke wanted it clearly understood that any change in the constitution had been and should be undertaken "upon the principles of reference to antiquity."[66] Radicals would have it that the Revolution of 1688 had been a departure from the past, and in that respect analogous to the French revolution they so admired. Burke contradicted them flatly: "The Revolution was made to preserve our *antient* indisputable laws and liberties, and that *antient* constitution of government which is our only security for law and liberty."[67] Just as the constitution, with its gaze fastened upon antiquity, was a prescriptive constitution, so too property came under the same sanction. Liberty and property were mutually supportive to the degree that they became almost indistinguishable in Burke's later thought, and the same principle secured them both.

In February 1790, Burke received a letter from an acquaintance inclined to be favorable to developments in France and to justify the confiscations of church property. Burke answered him with a short correspondence course on the subject of prescription.

It is not calling the landed estates, possessed by old *prescriptive rights,* the "accumulations of ignorance and superstition," that can support me shaking that grand title, which supersedes all other title, and which all my studies of general jurisprudence have taught me to consider as one principal cause of the formation of states; I mean the ascertaining and securing *prescription.* But these are donations made in "ages of ignorance and superstition." Be it so. It proves that these donations were made long ago; and this is *prescription;* and this gives right and title. It is possible that many estates about you were originally obtained by arms, that is, by violence, a thing almost as bad as superstition, and not much short of ignorance: but it is *old violence;* and that which might be wrong in the beginning, is consecrated by time, and becomes lawful. This may be superstition in me, and ignorance; but I had rather remain in ignorance and superstition than be enlightened and purified out of the first principles of law and natural justice.[68]

Burke's commitment was unshakable: "I can never be taught any thing else by *reason.   .   .   ."*[69]

Government was a contrivance of *human* wisdom to provide for human wants. Its ultimate source, however, was divine. For Burke, "He who gave our nature to be perfected by our virtue, willed also the necessary means of its perfection—He willed therefore the state—He willed its connexion with the source and original archetype of all perfection."[70] Any individual state was nothing more than "a clause in the great primaeval contract of eternal society, linking the lower with the higher natures, connecting the visible and invisible world, according to a fixed compact sanctioned by the inviolable oath which holds all physical and all moral natures, each in their appointed place. This law is not subject to the will of those, who by an obligation above them, and infinitely superior, are bound to submit their will to that law."[71] To do violence to any state was, not to put too fine an edge on it, to defy the will of the creator of the universe.

Modification, however, was permissible. Indeed, governments which lacked the means of making necessary and appropriate adjustments with the change of historical conditions doomed themselves. But "correction" always went hand in hand with "preservation," which meant that it was a slow process. Effects were calculated with care, studied with caution. It was especially important to see that "reformation" did not cost a price far greater than the advantage sought. "We compensate, we reconcile, we balance."[72] The legislator must take into account the perversities and frailities of human nature. Perfection makes no part of the plans. Obviously, the responsibility for such delicate tasks could not be allowed to fall upon impatient amateurs or men who cited as their qualification and right to govern the fact that they were men.

Nowhere did the revolutionaries betray their ineptitude more than in a lust for "perfect" system and regularity. Louis XVI's predecessors had put together his realm over centuries, gradually adding a principality here by conquest, a dukedom there by a politic marriage. The several provinces of France each had their own histories, customs, dialects, chartered privileges. The revolutionaries, in the interest of administrative efficiency, had ignored these differentiations and reordered the country into eighty-odd roughly equal jurisdictions, known as "departments," all centralized under the Parisian government. For Burke, this was government "with no better apparatus than the metaphysics of an under-graduate, and the mathematics and arithmetic of an exciseman." It overlooked peculiarities, it denied the sacred accidents of history. It fell drastically short of the wisdom of the "coarse husbandman" who knew enough to discriminate among sheep, horses, and oxen and not work and feed them all as though they were merely "animals." It was no minor matter, of course, that the French scheme was not so very different in spirit from what the English parliamentary reformers would have brought about. The same Burke who had been alarmed by their demands in the 1780s could ask in 1790: "When did you hear in Great Britain of any province suffering from its representation; what district from having no representation at all."[73]

A free government had also to be a stable government, and political stability presupposed social stability—the security of existing property rights. Here prejudice was crucial; without its hold, the multitudes were at the mercy of subversive doctrine. For all his confidence in the *Reflections* about the power of prejudice, however, there can be little doubt that he feared for its durability. He was deeply disturbed by the rise of popular radicalism in English over the previous twenty years and by the ominous enthusiasm for the French Revolution. Perhaps the unthinking commitment to the traditional constitution was coming unglued. After all, it had happened in France, where clever orators and the "Political Men of Letters" had rooted up faith in the old ways. It is no surprise that Burke, one of the greatest virtuosos ever to play upon the keyboard of our language, understood the persuasive power of words. "The social nature of man impels him to propagate his principles, as much as physical impulses urge him to propagate his kind."[74] Let false doctrines be spread about in the land, and chances were, Burke seemed to think, they would be believed. Just try talking sense to a beggar who had gotten wind of the rights of men: "Were he to say to a man, 'I have a good house, excellent cattle, fine furniture, pictures, tapestry, laces, plate, and delicious fare, but—you want your dinner'; he was apprehensive that he should find some difficulty in convincing him, that the superfluities recounted ought not to be employed in the relief of his necessities."[75]

Burke, of course, was not writing for beggars. The subtlety and richness of his prose were crafted for a highly educated audience, for the ruling class which he feared was being seduced by appearances in France. The responsibility for maintaining prejudice lay not with the poor, whom Burke preferred not to think at all, but with his social equals and especially his social betters—the only persons likely to make their way with ease through the densely packed arguments of the *Reflections*.

The "monied interest" was perhaps a threat to be contended with. Certainly in France it had done great damage, and Burke's analysis of the origins of the revolution reads for all the world like an anticipation of the Marxist version. As it turned out, however, the urban middle-class elements had been the real shock troops, dismantling clerical and aristocratic property only to be despoiled in their own turn. However much Burke worried about the monied interest, his eyes never strayed far from all those hair-dressers and tallow-chandlers. In the concluding passage to the *Reflections,* he resorted to a traditional explanation and rationalization of the place of the poor:

To keep a balance between the power of acquisition on the part of the subject and the demands he is to answer on the part of the state is the fundamental part of the skill of a true politician. The means of acquisition are prior in time and in arrangement. Good order is the foundation of all good things. To be enabled to acquire, the people, without being servile, must be tractable and obedient. The magistrate must have his reverence,

the laws their authority. The body of the people must not find the principles of natural subordination rooted out of their minds. They must labor
to obtain what by labor can be obtained; and when they find, as they
commonly do, the success disproportioned to the endeavor, they must be
taught their consolation in the final proportions of eternal justice. Of this
consolation whoever deprives them deadens their industry, and strikes at
the root of all acquisition as of all conservation. He that does this is the
cruel oppressor, the merciless enemy of the poor and wretched; at the same
time that by his wicked speculations he exposes the fruits of successful
industry and the accumulations of fortune to the plunder of the negligent,
the disappointed and the unprosperous.[76]

The Force of Familiarity

Long since enshrined as a "classic" of political philosophy, *Reflections on the Revolution in France* is surely more unlike traditional
philosophy than almost any other work in the category. Nothing
seemed to interest Burke less than logical progression, orderly sets
of deductions or inferences, reasoned refutations of opposing points
of view. His book is full of assertions, but little proof. How do we
know that "Each contract of each particular state is but a clause in
the great primaeval contract of eternal society . . . ?" Why should
we believe that it is *"natural"* to feel horrified at the events of 6
October 1789? What evidence is there that "man is by his constitution a religious animal; that atheism is against not only our reason
but our instincts; and that it cannot prevail long"?[77] Confronted by
arguments with which he disagreed, as often as not Burke dismissed
them with ridicule. The revolutionaries were wrong because they
held mistaken principles—the abstractions of the "rights of men"
But Burke was just as liable to heap abuse upon them as debate
with them, and his pages are full of angry epithets: "creeping sy-
cophants," "mechanic philosophy," "Jews and jobbers," "country
attornies and obscure curates," "stock-jobbing constitution," "meta-
physic declarations," "ignoble oligarchy," "a mob (excuse the term,
it is still in use here)."

It may be too much to demand reportorial accuracy from such a
temperament, and Burke did not provide it. While his sources of
information regarding France were probably often at fault, still
Burke often presented rhetoric designed to persuade rather than
simply inform in the guise of descriptive accounts. His treatment
of the October Days was largely fanciful. His sketch of the French

nobility, supposedly based in part upon his trip to the Continent in 1773, speaks for itself:

On my best observation, compared with my best enquiries, I found your nobility for the greater part composed of men of an high spirit, and of a delicate sense of honour, both with regard to themselves individually, and with regard to their whole corps, over whom they kept, beyond what is common in other countries, a censorial eye. They were tolerably well-bred; very officious, humane, and hospitable; in their conversation frank and open; with a good military tone; and reasonably tinctured with literature, particularly of the authors in their own language. Many had pretensions far above this description. . . .

As to their behaviour to the inferior classes, they appeared to me to comport themselves towards them with good-nature, and with something more nearly approaching to familiarity, than is generally practised with us in the intercourse between the higher and lower ranks of life. To strike any person, even in the most abject condition, was at thing in a manner unknown, and would be highly disgraceful. Instances of other ill-treatment of the humble part of the community were rare; and as to attacks made upon the property or the personal liberty of the commons, I never heard of any whatsoever from *them*. . . .[78]

Even as largely undocumented assertion, the central social argument of the *Reflections* has its problems. This is not to measure Burke against sophisticated modern scholarship, but merely against standards of plausibility and consistency which ought to be at least recognizable in any time. One problem is that, like the Marxist versions of the revolution, Burke identifies few historical actors, few individuals of consequence. The revolution is made by groups, faceless social categories animated by predictable motives for their station—greed, ambition, pride, resentment, and so forth. There are no *people* in Burke's National Assembly, merely litigious notaries, stupid clerics, and the like. As a result, his account of the revolution becomes nearly as abstract as the philosophy he so detested. The *Reflections* is reminiscent of those histories written in terms of "forces" and "factors," bereft of real human beings engaging in concrete actions. Such accounts may entertain, but they can never convince.

In the same vein, Burke's anonymous actors are dreadfully stereotyped. There is the radiant queen, the tragic king, the lustrous nobility ("the Corinthian capital of polished society"),[79] not to count a few base traitors; serried against them are the grasping lawyers, the scheming financiers, the perfidious *philosophes,* and of course the gullible ranks of the low and feeble, panting to be tempted away from their rightful subordination, never far from donning the gruesome mask of the swinish multitude. Except for those few renegade peers, nobody ever steps out of character. It is all too pat, and at some distance from the complexity of human affairs which Burke claimed to appreciate.

For the most part, Burke's villains are obvious enough, but even he could not always keep them straight. It looks at first as though the lawyers and the parish priests in the National Assembly are to blame for France's torment. But then we learn that it was the monied interest, with an assist from the political men of letters, who prepared the way for the revolution by subverting respect for social and political authority. The monied interest planned to destroy the aristocracy, first of all by despoiling the church. But why, then, were these men of suspect wealth such a small component in the Assembly?[80] And how, with such a tiny clique at the center of power, were they able to gain their goals? Burke has difficulty deciding which revolutionaries caused the most damage, those whose fault it was that they owned no property, or those who owned the wrong sort of property. The monied men made the revolution possible and were later its first principal beneficiaries; in between, however, they disappear from view, and leave Burke's case confused and inconsistent.

As against these shortcomings, the *Reflections* of course has its virtues, not the least of which is its prose. Probably no other document in the history of political philosophy offers so much literary satisfaction. The rolling periodic sentences have an overpowering rhythm and Burke packed them with almost incredibly rich imagery. His awesome gift for abuse sticks in the mind every bit as much as his philosophical principles:

I see the confiscators begin with bishops, and chapters, and monasteries; but I do not see them end there. I see the princes of the blood, who, by the oldest usages of that kingdom, held large landed estates, (hardly with the compliment of a debate) deprived of their possessions, and in lieu of their stable independent property, reduced to the hope of some precarious, charitable pension, at the pleasure of an assembly, which of course will pay little regard to the rights of pensioners at pleasure, when it despises those of legal proprietors. Flushed with the insolence of their first inglorious victories, and pressed by the distresses caused by their lust of unhallowed lucre, disappointed but not discouraged, they have at length ventured completely to subvert all property of all descriptions throughout the extent of a great kingdom. They have compelled all men, in all transactions of commerce, in the disposal of lands, in civil dealing, and throughout the whole communion of life, to accept as perfect payment and good and lawful tender, the symbols of their speculations on a projected sale of their plunder. What vestiges of liberty or property have they left? The tenant-right of a cabbage-garden, a year's interest in a hovel, the good-will of an ale-house, or a baker's shop, the very shadow of a constructive property, are more ceremoniously treated in our parliament than with you the oldest and most valuable landed possessions, in the hands of the most respectable personages, or than the whole body of the monied and commercial interest of your country.[81]

Burke's rhetorical concision, the aptness and succinctness of his images, his manipulation of mood, his feel for rhythm were never in better control—or applied to a better subject—than in the *Reflections*. It was humanistic, and laced with high moral tragedy. It was Burke's *Lear,* his *Paradise Lost*—both works he warmly admired.

But style aside, and without entering into discussion of the merit of Burke's political ideas, the greatest strength of the *Reflections* was its lack of originality. Burke attacked the revolution, and defended English society and the constitution, on grounds which were not exotic but wholly familiar: social inequality, the rule of an elite, the avoidance of extremes, the dangers of democracy, the sanctity of property, the rightness of religion. He was not so much trying to convince his readers as to *remind* them of what they already believed, or at any rate ought to have believed. It was the familiarity of his arguments which gave them their force, and gave Burke his conviction in stating them. It is that air of conviction, indeed of passionate commitment to the fundamental values of his society, which gave Burke's voice the power to stir long after that society disappeared.

Chapter Six
Counterrevolutionary Crusade

The last six and one-half years of Burke's life were a time of considerable literary productivity. He wrote eight substantial pamphlets, and though none of them approached the *Reflections* in importance, the French revolution was central to them all. Burke did not much alter his views on the revolution, though he shifted his emphasis from time to time and in response to events. If anything, he became more strident.

Gallic Tumult

Early in 1791, Burke fired off a letter to a member of the French National Assembly who had dared a rejoinder to the *Reflections*. Immediately, Burke sounded the theme of government by the wrong people:

I can never be convinced that the scheme of placing the highest powers of the state in church-wardens and constables and other such officers, guided by the prudence of litigious attorneys and Jew brokers, and set in action by shameless women of the lowest condition, by keepers of hotels, taverns, and brothels, by pert apprentices, by clerks, shop-boys, hairdressers, fiddlers, and dancers on the stage (who, in such a commonwealth as yours, will in future overbear, as already they have overborne, the sober incapacity of dull, uninstructed men, of useful, but laborious occupations,) can never be put into any shape that must not be both disgraceful and destructive.[1]

Burke continued with page after page of this vituperation, excoriating the "whole gang of usurers, peddlers, and itinerant Jew discounters," the "dancing masters, fiddlers, pattern-drawers, friseurs, and valets-de-chambre" he was convinced were taking over France. Rousseau, who had come in for only passing savagery in the *Reflections,* now became the principal inspiration for a philosophy of leveling. Burke concluded with a reminder that a people deserve liberty just in so far as they are ready to restrain their own appetites, as the French were so manifestly unable to do. "It is ordained in the eternal constitution of things, that men of intemperate minds cannot be free. Their passions forge their fetters."[2]

At the end of that same year, Burke momentarily transformed the social aspect of the revolution into a means for attaining a political end—the establishment of political democracy. Since men of property would be the staunchest opponents of majority rule, their removal became the revolution's first tactical objective.[3] A letter to a French correspondent in 1793 returned the focus to property. Every last domino which the revolutionaries had toppled would have to be set up again, right back to the first one whose fall had occasioned so much grief—the estates of the church. Otherwise, Burke gave government and property in the rest of Europe no more than twenty years of security; the following year he reduced the estimate to ten.[4] In the final pamphlet of his life, Burke consolidated all these views and concluded that the revolution was equally pledged to war on monarchy, property, and religion.[5]

For Burke, the revolution never really changed its face, it only put on different masks now and then, each of them as repulsive as the last. In the *Reflections*, he had analyzed its early stages and on their basis projected a future of civil war and anarchy for France. When that future came to pass, Burke felt justified in his predictions. Repeatedly in the 1790s, he returned to the period from July to November 1789—from the outburst, that is, of the "old Parisian ferocity" to the confiscation of the church's estates—to pinpoint the deadly source of the revolution's evil. Its destructive tendencies were intrinsic; it careened toward chaos as though directed by an inner logic dictated by its parentage and the circumstances of its birth.

Each new convulsion in France seemed to bear Burke out. In retrospect, however, we may ask whether Burke was right for the right reasons, for there is an aroma of determinism about his views which ought to raise suspicions in all observers of the past. It is manifestly true that France suffered another revolution in 1792 and civil war for some time thereafter. But did these developments stem directly and unavoidably from the events of 1789?

In 1790, Burke was already referring to France as a republic in fact, so emasculated did he regard the crown. As a matter of fact, the monarchy retained powers of real substance if not epic scope. The principal limitations which the National Assembly placed upon the crown were the establishment of a countervailing legislature, the promise of a constitution by which the king must abide, and the granting to him of a suspensive rather than an absolute veto. There was no discernible interest in republicanism, still widely held as an unsuitable government for large states and best restricted to places like Geneva or Venice. Democracy, at least in the form of universal adult male suffrage, had a few partisans, but the Assembly ignored them and attached a property qualification to the vote for future elections. After the initial upheaval, France was relatively calm for two years.

The persistent royalism of the Assembly is especially notable in the face of Louis XVI's uncooperative attitude. He chafed under the limitations upon his prerogative and longed to see the revolution and all its works obliterated. In June 1791, he attempted secretly to spirit the royal family out of the country; from exile, he would invite his "loyal subjects" to send the politicians packing, their constitution with them, whereupon he would return to the throne under more agreeable conditions. Captured before reaching the border, the royal family was herded back to Paris in ignominy. If the Assembly had wished, nothing would have been easier than punishment for this egregious show of bad faith. The constitution was completed, but it had yet to be formally enacted. The crown might have been stripped of further powers. So little was the Assembly inclined to weaken monarchy further, however, that it did not act.

What undid the monarchy and disrupted the civil peace was not doctrine, nor was it dancing-masters. It was war, upon which France entered in the spring of 1792 and which lasted, with only brief parentheses of peace, for twenty-three years. The war arose from numerous causes, too complicated for detailed treatment here. The National Assembly and its successor, the Legislative Assembly, which first sat in September 1791, had its share of missionary zealots who would spread the benefits of their revolution to the oppressed brethren of neighboring lands. There were also expansionists of a more familiar sort, interested in sheer territorial aggrandizement. Some suffered from panic: they feared that Europe's monarchs would try to snuff out the revolution before its sparks drifted dangerously outside French frontiers. In such circumstances, perhaps the best course was a preemptive strike. Others suffered equally from cynicism: lusting for ministerial office, they sought to generate enthusiasm for war and advertise its advantages so that, if and when it came, they would be the natural persons upon whom to call for leadership.

All these elements combined in early 1792 to throw France into war against Prussia and Austria. The immediate results were catastrophic. Aristocratic emigration had thinned out the French officer corps substantially; for two years, the Assembly's preoccupation with domestic questions had afforded little time for attention to military organization and supply. Suddenly, the French found the enemy had penetrated deeply into their own territory. Defeat in war surely meant not only political reprisals but the end of the revolutionary institutions. The Emperor Leopold of Austria had never been wildly excited about war with France; but now that it had come, he would certainly take the opportunity of victory to turn back the calendar to at least 1788, if for no other reason than that Queen Marie Antoinette was his sister.

Military defeat, economic deprivation, and a mounting crisis of morale characterized the early months of war. At the same time, however, it was becoming clear that the war had placed Louis XVI in an impossible situation. As commander-in-chief, his duty was to prosecute the struggle with all possible vigor. As a monarch shackled by a despised constitution, his personal interest was to see the national enemy rout his own armies. This inescapable contradiction was appreciated in Paris, the center of revolutionary sentiment and patriotic ardor. The choice was between the revolution and the monarchy, so long supposed to have been compatible. By the end of August 1792, the royal family was under lock and key, government documents no longer referred to Louis with a roman numeral after his name, and France was a republic.

It is difficult to see what any of this owes to storming the Bastille or reading too much Rousseau. The war was doubtless a gargantuan error on France's part, but nothing that happened in 1789 appears to have entailed that the mistake would be made. The war was a foolish accident which could have been avoided, just as the National Assembly wished to avoid republicanism. Once begun, however, there was nothing for it but to fight to a successful conclusion. This was even the opinion of some of the war's most vocal opponents, such as Maximilien Robespierre, who had sat in the National Assembly and was thereafter a journalist and prominent member of the Jacobin Club. Before April 1792, Robespierre had claimed that the war was a pointless diversion from the many domestic problems which remained to be solved. Afterwards, with the revolution in danger, Robespierre became one of the most prominent spokesmen for a total war effort.

It was that effort which led directly to civil war. The Convention, the new republican legislature elected in September 1792, soon called for complete commitment and unbounded sacrifice from the populace. The initial response was gratifying but difficult to sustain. Mass conscription and mounting confiscations to supply the troops did not sit well with provincial regions remote from the war and from the imperious capital which governed by decree. Many people were horrified in January 1793 when Louis was sentenced to the guillotine. The increasing assertiveness of the radical Parisian crowds worried people in the hinterland. Before long, civil war was born of weariness with foreign war, antagonism with Parisian "despotism" (not a new sentiment in the revolutionary era), and a conviction that the revolution had gone "too far."

The government met those insurgents, located primarily in the south, southeast, and the west, with a repression which was unquestionably awful. Again, however, it is difficult to see this so-called reign of terror as a predictable outgrowth of 1789. Most governments, however they may have gained power, treat armed insurrection in approximately the same way; the British response to periodic Irish uprisings over the years is merely one case in point. Civil insurgents would have received rough handling in France under any conditions, whether or not anyone had laid a finger on the property of the church.

If Burke never understood the real significance of the war for France, still he grasped that its coming brought a change. In the *Reflections,* the revolution was a danger largely because of the example it set, the harm which its very existence might do to long-standing English prejudice. A year later, as talk of war ran through Paris, he took the revolution for one *"of doctrine and theoretic dogma . . . in which proselytism makes an essential part."*[6] France would become an arsenal upon which its sympathizers everywhere would draw for weapons to spread the revolution. Burke was not ready to sit idly by while madmen tore down society around his ears. The forces of counterrevolution which remained within France were too weak to act alone; Europe would have to aid them.

Once war finally came, England—to Burke's irritation—took nearly a year to join the anti-French coalition. Pitt, no friend of the revolution, had been prepared to recognize that English interests were involved only when France posed a strategic threat by moving into Belgium. To Burke, this was a narrow construction of "interest." He saw the French as fanatical propagators of their revolution. War with them was *"a religious war,"* a struggle with "armed doctrine."[7]

Essentially, Burke was confusing—and he would not be the last to do so—revolutionary zeal with nationalism. In part, they overlapped; besides, nationalism was new enough in continental Europe that Burke's confusion is understandable. French popular support for the war, though very far indeed from total, was still greater and more ferocious than anything in living memory. The defense of revolutionary institutions and of an independent motherland engaged popular sympathies in a way which the earlier dynastic wars of the eighteenth century never could have done. But the point remains that this profound, even desperate, commitment was primarily defensive. It reached its highest pitch when allied troops had their greatest success. The terror, conceived as confiscations and price regulations and all the other instrumentalities of total warfare along with violent coercion, was primarily a policy of defense. When the French finally turned the tide in 1794, the Convention was ready to discard this expedient as having served its purpose. Robespierre, by then in a position of power, insisted upon keeping the machinery of terror intact; the Convention overthrew him and had his head in the bargain.

When the French war effort became one of expansion, it tended to look far more like earlier struggles than Burke could see. The principal objects became territory, strategic advantage, and plunder—the latter undertaken not to destroy undemocratic social systems but to help pay for the war. The war dragged on for what were traditional reasons, not because it was a holy war which could only end with the republicanization of the world. When the allies occupied French territory, peace could only be made on terms detrimental to France's national interest as the government perceived it. When French armies moved the battlefronts across their own boundaries, the prospect of further conquest was too tempting to pass up. Sometimes the French attempted to plant their own new institutions, or versions of them, in conquered territories; this practice was far more common, however, under that most unrevolutionary of rulers, Napoleon, than under the republic.

Indeed, if we must find fanaticism in the war, Burke's own brand had few competitors. Military victory would have been but a prelude to the crucial features of his own war aims. Then must come the *complete* restoration of all property which had changed hands since 1789 to its "rightful" owners. No trace of revolutionary institutions could remain, and Burke would root their architects out of positions of authority, one and all, bag and baggage. Exiled priests and nobles would return to undertake the work of "reanimating the loyalty, fidelity, and religion of the people." In the towns, he hoped, enough men of "gravity and property" were still about to "restrain and regulate the seditious rabble there, as the gentlemen will on their own estates."[8] Without reestablishing the security of hereditary property and the dignity of hereditary rank, the restoration of hereditary monarchy—*"the main object of the war"*—would not last long. For all this, however, Burke's interest was not to punish most Frenchmen, but to convert them, to bring them back from the dangerous idiocy of the "rights of men" and the orgy of pillage to a wholesome respect for social hierarchy and traditional authority. He would listen to no·talk of peace which stopped short of this radical restoration. There was no compromising with regicides, Jacobins, and atheists. To leave them any breath at all was to tempt them to rise again and reinvigorate as well their numerous foreign sympathizers. The revolution must be smashed to smithereens, plowed under, and salt strewn where it had stood.

These proposals may seem incongruous coming from the longtime spokesman of moderation and compromise, the opponent of "perfection" and "extremes." But caution in policy was Burke's rule when operating *within* traditional constitutions. The French had wiped the slate clean, had thought themselves returning to a juridical "state of nature" where they could write anew. Theirs was not "old violence"; they could not claim the sanction of prescription for their innovations. It was to return to a traditional situation that Burke advocated extreme measures.

But the war dragged on too long for root-and-branch restoration to be feasible. There was no meaningful peace until 1815, and by that time the sale of church property and of confiscated émigré estates had been going on for nearly a quarter century. Bonaparte knew better than to stir these sleeping dogs, and so did the Bourbon monarchy once it returned in 1814—although the Bourbons also indemnified many nobles for their losses out of public funds. Had Burke realized how long it would be before restoration could take place, perhaps prudence would have got the better part of him.

Rupture in Whigdom

Even before the war, Burke's first concern with the revolution was not its depredations abroad, but its dangers at home. As always, when France and England were at war, there was danger in Ireland. The French, Burke worried, would exploit dissatisfaction there in order to get a military foothold. Thus it was imperative to proceed with reform and especially religious toleration. He saw the Roman Catholic religion as "the most effectual Barrier, if not the sole Barrier, against Jacobinism" in Ireland. The revolutionaries would seek "to eradicate prejudice out of the minds of men . . ." Only a secure and flourishing Catholicism would keep it rooted there.[9] Yet an even more immediate threat was present in England itself.

Reflections on the Revolution in France appeared on 1 November 1790. Some 7,000 copies sold within a week, 5,000 more by the end of the month. By the time of Burke's death in 1797, there had been perhaps 18,000 domestic sales alone, as well as several foreign translations.[10] The book also prompted numerous rejoinders, especially from English radicals, such as Tom Paine's *The Rights of Man,* James Mackintosh's *Vindiciae Gallicae,* and, a few years later, William Godwin's *Political Justice.* Of these three, Paine's was certainly the most popular and deserves at least brief attention.

The Rights of Man appeared in two parts, the first in 1791 and the second a year later. Paine, the English artisan who had come to journalistic prominence during the American revolution as an advocate of democracy, claimed to have written an answer to Burke, but in fact he said relatively little that was directly responsive. He did seize on a handful of Burke's arguments and attempt to demolish them. The notion of an hereditary constitution, for instance, struck him as absurd:

Every generation is, and must be, competent to all the purposes which its occasions require. It is the living, and not the dead, that are to be accommodated. When man ceases to be, his power and his wants cease with him; and having no longer any participation in the concerns of this

world, he has no longer any authority in directing who shall be its governors, or how its government shall be organized, or how administered.[11]

It followed that such hereditary institutions as aristocracy made no
sense, and Paine belabored Burke on his nostalgia for the demise
of aristocratic chivalry in a nation whose real problems were the
widespread misery of the commons: "He pities the plumage, but
forgets the dying bird."[12] Indeed, Paine was not above misquoting
Burke in order to make him appear the knave in the guise of a
fool.[13]

But Paine understood at whom Burke had directed the *Reflections,*
and he had no interest in competing for that audience. Instead, he
was trying to reach the hair-dressers and tallow-chandlers, the disen-
franchised whom Burke would keep that way. *The Rights of Man* is
a plain, even homely book, its arguments straightforward, its French
phrases considerately translated. Paine was attempting neither to
convert Burke and men like him nor to refute the *Reflections* at every
juncture. *The Rights of Man* is an alternative manifesto, sounding
the call that men have innate rights *as men,* that they do not sacrifice
these rights when they form a society. "Man did not enter into
society to become *worse* than he was before, nor to have fewer rights
than he had before, but to have those rights better secured."[14] Paine,
like Burke, was writing not a work of systematic philosophy, but
an appeal, a partisan statement of democratic republicanism. He
joined argument with his antagonist far less often than he stated a
flatly contrary proposition.

Burke's intention, of course, had not been to win over the radicals—whom in any case he considered fundamentally ineducable—
any more than it had been merely to berate Frenchmen. The audience
he wished first of all to reach was composed largely of those Englishmen of property and standing who either paid no mind to the
French revolution or, worse still, applauded what they saw as healthy
change proceeding according to sound principles. Though he must
have been gratified by the commercial success of the *Reflections,* as
his personal finances were in chronic disrepair, he had plainly written
not for the masses but for the elite. Indeed, given the choice of but
a few persons who alone might be allowed to read the book, Burke
would probably have chosen certain of his own fellow Whigs.

Twenty years earlier, Burke had defended the Rockingham Whigs
first of all on the grounds that they were united by certain principles.

To whatever degree that may have been true, it became less so in the years after the marquis's death in 1782, when indisputable leadership of the party failed to devolve upon any single person. Common political interest promoted a semblance of unity during the early years of the Hastings affair and the Regency crisis, but the coming of the French revolution revealed deep fissures among the Whigs. The central figure in the subsequent disputes, along with Burke, was Charles James Fox, an accomplished orator, an ambitious politician, and a long-standing friend of Burke's though twenty years his junior.

Fox was a man of somewhat elastic principles, even by the rubbery standards of eighteenth-century politics. Throughout the American war, he stood with the Rockinghams in opposition and fired countless shafts of verbal abuse into Lord North's leathery hide. Early in the 1780s, however, Fox and North joined to form a coalition government. When the king and his rational faculties momentarily went their separate ways at the end of 1788, Fox was confident that his own close friendship with the Prince of Wales would propel him to the head of a new government; when his vision failed to materialize, he was deeply disappointed. Seeking some fulcrum for moving the unbudgeable Pitt, Fox cultivated his good relations with democratic reformers and hailed the early stages of the French revolution just when Burke was beginning to harbor the darkest doubts.

Early in 1790, the House of Commons considered an appropriations bill for the army. Given developments across the English Channel, Burke was anxious to have an adequate armed force on hand. Fox failed to see any danger and argued for cuts in the army in order to save money. Later that year, Fox and his associate, Richard Sheridan, put forward a measure that would have virtually abolished civil restrictions upon nonconformists in England. But as a number of Protestant dissenters were prominent in the growing movement of pro-French radicals, Burke decided that the expansion of religious toleration was not timely. It meant an open break with Sheridan, although Burke and Fox maintained relations.

They would not do so for long. The political atmosphere was polarizing. Burke had received much praise for the *Reflections,* but Whigs sympathetic to Fox's views had also attacked Burke on the grounds that he had betrayed the classic Whiggism of which he had been such an eloquent advocate for twenty-five years. Although

Burke kept his peace on the subject in the House for some months, he was by no means squeamish about a confrontation between Whigs of his own persuasion, whose nominal leader was the Duke of Portland, and those who looked to Fox and Sheridan. Finally, on 6 May 1791, Burke chose to restate his position on the revolution before the Commons. Inevitably, as Fox defended his own views, the debate took a personal turn, and Burke ended up by publicly renouncing an old and intimate friendship while Fox stood in tears.

The party in whose cause Burke had labored all his political life was now badly split. On questions involving the revolution and its English implications, such as parliamentary reform, the Whig division had the effect of further weakening the opposition and delivering an important group of votes over to Pitt's antirevolutionary majority. (Formal coalition did not come until 1794, when at Burke's insistent urging, members of Portland's faction joined the government.) Naturally, the split did nothing to silence Foxite claims that Burke had betrayed his Whig principles. These charges carried a particular sting for Burke precisely because he saw himself clarifying and affirming traditional Whiggism in the face of mindless enthusiasm for a revolution which defied the essence of the Revolution Settlement itself.

Moreover, it is important to remember that Burke's Whig accusers were no collection of church-wardens and valets-de-chambre. They were men of wealth and impressive social position, and Burke could not fathom why they should wish "to propagate the principles of French Levelling and confusion, by which no house is safe from its Servants, and no Officer from his Soldiers, and no State or constitution from conspiracy and insurrection."[15] Had he lived in a later century, he might have resorted to the term "radical chic." As it was, he sprang to his own defense in a pamphlet published in August 1791, *An Appeal from the New to the Old Whigs,* which sought to establish that any deviation from "old" Whig principles had not been on his part.

In the *Appeal,* Burke attempted to establish the nature of old Whiggism, as it had taken shape in the revolution of 1688 and thereafter, and to show that it found its contemporary expression more in his principles than in those of the Foxes and Sheridans. Moreover, he went to some lengths to argue the consistency of his own political position over the preceding quarter century. The most interesting parts of the book, however, are his attempts to define the new Whigs. "The whole scheme of our mixed constitution is to prevent any one of its principles from being carried as far as, taken by itself and theoretically, it would go."[16] The new Whigs contradicted that scheme and sought, according to Burke, "the perfections of extreme" by exalting the "popular" part of the constitution—that embodied in the elected House of Commons—into the dominant element. Their philosophy, borrowed of course from France, preached not merely the original but also the enduring and even inalienable sovereignty of the people. It made of a popular majority an omnipotent agent which could undo existing government and dismiss its magistrates at will.

This "appeal" of the new Whigs failed to appreciate that the contract of government imposed mutual obligations. While the governors were obliged to regard the welfare of the people as a whole, the governed were equally obliged to obey the authorities. The people had a solemn and unshakable duty to accept their constituted government, *even if* they themselves had not constituted it. Choice simply did not enter into the matter: "Men without their choice derive benefits from that association [under government]; without their choice they are subjected to duties in consequence of these benefits; and without their choice they enter into a virtual obligation as binding as it is actual."[17] It was a matter of duty, and not of voluntary acceptance, precisely because the arrangements of government were a matter of Divine and not human will. People in society are "disposed and marshaled" by God; they are assigned roles and relationships which "are not matters of choice."[18]

Men do not act "as a people"—that is, with the authority of the whole—when they are simply the numerical majority within their society. In order so to act, they must "be in that state of habitual social discipline in which the wiser, the more expert, and the more opulent conduct, and by conducting enlighten and protect, the weaker, the less knowing, and the less provided with the goods of fortune."[19] In other words, we are back in the land of "presumptive virtue" and the leadership of a "true natural aristocracy." In contrast to the *Reflections,* Burke here offers a detailed account of why we may presume virtue of persons of a certain social background, and the passage is instructive, for it shows that more elevated principles than class fear and material selfishness moved him:

To be bred, in a place of estimation; to see nothing low and sordid from
one's infancy; to be taught to respect one's self; to be habituated to the
censorial inspection of the public eye; to look early to public opinion; to
stand upon such elevated ground as to be enabled to take a large view of
the widespread and infinitely diversified combinations of men and affairs
in a large society; to have leisure to read, to reflect, to converse; to be
enabled to draw the court and attention of the wise and learned, wherever
they are to be found; to be habituated in armies to command and to obey;
to be taught to despise danger in the pursuit of honor and duty; to be
formed to the greatest degree of vigilance, foresight, and circumspection
in a state of things in which no fault is committed with impunity and
the slightest mistakes draw on the most ruinous consequences; to be led
to a guarded and regulated conduct, from a sense that you are considered
as an instructor of your fellow citizens in their highest concerns, and that
you act as a reconciler between God and man; to be employed as an
administrator of law and justice, and to be thereby amongst the first
benefactors to mankind; to be a professor of high science, or of liberal and
ingenuous art; to be amongst rich traders, who from their success are
presumed to have sharp and vigorous understandings, and to possess the
virtues of diligence, order, constancy, and regularity, and to have cultivated a habitual regard to commutative justice—these are the circumstances of men that form what I should call a "natural" aristocracy, without
which there is no nation.[20]

From this sentence, it emerges that Burke supported aristocratic
rule neither from slavishness to social betters nor from a thoughtless
devotion to the status quo. It may well be mistaken that one could
presume England's governing elite to share in all or even many of
these advantages; but, at least by eighteenth-century measures, advantages they surely were. Burke's vision of an elite was not, therefore, simply a vision of money; it encompassed some of the more
socially useful things that money can buy.

It was when a society was under the firm leadership of men who
had accumulated such experiences that it could be said to act "as a
people," or better yet, be truly in "a state of Nature": "For man is
by nature reasonable, and he is never perfectly in his natural state
but when he is placed where reason may be best cultivated and most
predominates."[21] Burke meant, of course, that man's reasonable
nature can assert itself only when virtuous leadership controls appetites and moderates the exercise of civil liberty. Let a majority of
the people act on its own, however, and it became little better than
a herd of wild beasts. Let it be guided by the principles of the

"rights of men," and there will be felt, "in all its aggravation, the pernicious consequence of destroying all docility in the minds of those who are not formed for finding their own way in the labyrinths of political theory."[22] As matters stood in 1791, people who would never dare to disassemble their own timepieces were confident they could take apart the infinitely complex gears and pinwheels of the constitution without doing any damage.

Burke was hard put to find any evidence that his pleadings were doing much good. Fox continued his dangerous dalliance with the revolution, and in 1793 Burke ticked off no less than fifty-four charges of misconduct against him.[23] Burke feared also that the English people's warm attachment to its prejudices which he had noted in the *Reflections* was further eroding. In his final years, he despaired in the conviction that of the roughly 400,000 voting citizens of England and Scotland, fully one-fifth were "pure Jacobins, utterly incapable of amendment, objects of eternal vigilance, and, when they break out, of legal constraint. On these, no reason, no argument, no example, no venerable authority, can have the slightest influence."[24] Any peace which stopped short of total victory and sweeping restoration in France played directly into the hands of this treacherous fifth column.[25] Events did nothing to moderate these jeremiads at the close of Burke's life. He continued to worry about the progress of revolutionary sentiments in England and the resolution of its governors to carry on the war to a proper conclusion. If Britain were to "perish," he wrote less than two months before he died himself, it would be not for a want of "material means of strength" but "by a poverty and imbecility of mind. . . ."[26]

The Final Battle

Burke felt that he was losing his last crusade, yet there was nothing new in that. Celebrated by posterity as one of the greatest figures in British parliamentary history, he rarely won more than a partial victory and often fell short of that. For years, his counsel on American policy received so little attention that—to use one of his own conceits—he might have had a lamppost for an interlocutor. There was progress toward statutory religious toleration, but even Burke himself ended up voting against extending it in his later years for political reasons. England suffered no abuses from a court "cabal," since one had never really existed; but a non-Whig majority persisted for a generation after his death. The concept of political party never received widespread approval in his lifetime. Ireland remained under severe restraints politically, economically, and religiously. The "economical reforms" eventually became law, but much truncated. The Commons impeached Hastings; the Lords acquitted him. Parliament averted reform in the eighteenth century, but the radical movement continued to grow impressively, though Burke's estimation as to its size was impressionistic at best.

Burke achieved fame and honor, but the rewards for his lengthy public service were principally intangible. From time to time, a stroke of good luck improved his personal finances, but frequently they traveled from the utterly bleak to the merely grim. He had the fiercest of family loyalties, and constantly plunged his own scant resources into schemes for enrichment concocted by his brother Richard and his "cousin" Will. Both turned out to be more adept at flirting with scandal than at making money and brought Edmund's own good name into jeopardy from time to time. In his brief stint as Paymaster of the Forces, Burke had the opportunity to enjoy the material advantages of office, and he did so, though hardly more piratcally than his contemporaries. Even so, he was in debt until nearly the end of his life.

As Burke's retirement from the House of Commons came in 1794, so too came some official recognition of his contributions. Pitt saw to it that he received three small pensions whose total value slightly exceeded £3,500. Even these gratifying gestures, which at least allowed Burke to put his personal finances in order before his death, did not pass to him untarnished. The Duke of Bedford, the young scion of the ancient Russell family who had been heard to speak approvingly of the French revolution, raised questions in the House of Lords as to whether Burke's public career really justified these grants. Burke answered in a pamphlet which appeared in 1796. It was his penultimate publication, and it summed up much of his political career and thought.

Burke was proud, injured, sixty-seven years old—more than twice Bedford's age. There was nothing to be gained by holding back, and the duke, his gentle birth notwithstanding, felt the lash of Burke's ripe polemical style. *A Letter to a Noble Lord* (not Bedford, but Burke's friend Baron Grenville) defended Burke's public career and especially the importance of his work on India and the "economical reforms," yet managed to maintain a constant reference to the French revolution. Was Burke's legislation modest? Perhaps, though it was to be kept in mind that *"To innovate is not to reform. The French revolutionists complained of everything; they refused to reform anything; and they left nothing, no, nothing at all unchanged."*[27]

Burke easily cast himself as the underdog in the quarrel, emphasizing his relatively humble origins in contrast to the vast wealth and impressive lineage of the duke. "I was not, like his Grace of Bedford, swaddled and rocked and dandled into a legislator. . . ." "At every step of my progress in life, (for in every step was I traversed and opposed,) and at every turnpike I met, I was obliged to show my passport, and again and again to prove my sole title to the honour of being useful to my country, by a proof that I was not wholly unacquainted with its laws and the whole system of its interests both abroad and at home. Otherwise, no rank, no toleration even, for me."[28]

With another turn of the screw, Bedford became the compleat hypocrite, for Burke went into scathing detail on the origins of the Russell family fortune—huge grants of land, far more valuable than Burke's pensions, detached by the odious Henry VIII from noble families which dared oppose him and given to the Russells for their loyalty. "The first of those immoderate grants was not taken from the ancient demesne of the crown, but from the recent confiscation of the ancient nobility of the land. The lion, having sucked the blood of his prey, threw the offal carcass to the jackal in waiting. Having tasted once the food of confiscation, the favourites became fierce and ravenous."[29] What made the Duke of Bedford think that only the House of Russell was worthy of royal favor? Why did he think that only Henry VIII could appreciate merit?

After dwelling briefly upon the loss of his son, and Burke did not pass up the opportunity to compare the duke unfavorably to Richard, Jr., he moved toward his conclusion. The Duke of Bedford enjoyed his material inheritance, Burke noted, largely because of its protection by the doctrine of prescription—a doctrine for whose recognition Burke took no small credit. Indeed, Bedford was in Burke's debt: "The Duke of Bedford will stand as long as prescriptive law endures. . . ."[30] But there was a challenge to its endurance, "the rude inroad of Gallic tumult, with its sophistical rights of man to falsify the account, and its sword as a make-weight to throw into the scale. . . ." If the duke sought, from principle or politics, to

pave the way for the revolutionaries in England, he would do well
to keep in mind that "Ingratitude to benefactors is the first of
revolutionary virtues."[31] He should understand that the revolutionaries "are the Duke of Bedford's natural hunters; and he is their
natural game."[32]

The double irony of Bedford's charges was not lost on Burke. He
had spent most of his adult life defending an aristocratic social
system, an aristocratic constitution, and an aristocratic political
party. When that aristocracy faced a frontal assault, one of its most
luminous representatives—and at that from a family of long-standing Whiggish tendencies—stepped forth to belittle the lookout who
had warned of the invasion. Burke, always something of an outsider,
remained one at the end.

Chapter Seven
Consistency and Conservatism

When the Foxite Whigs turned on Burke after the publication of the *Reflections,* one recurrent theme in the onslaught was that of his political consistency. Burke's detractors wondered publicly whatever had become of the courageous champion of American liberties, the critic of royal influence, the advocate of reform in subject Ireland. Where that man had once stood, they could see only a defender of established ways, eulogizing monarchy in France and prejudice in England. Burke answered these critics in the *Appeal,* but he failed to silence them either during his lifetime or in subsequent generations. The issue of his consistency has intrigued commentators in three centuries.

If, by consistency, one means utter uniformity of views in a literary and political career of more than forty years, then of course there is no point in searching for it because it is not there. Burke switched his position on a number of issues, for reasons ranging from understandable to highly dubious. At first, he had opposed government regulation of the East India Company on the ground that it would be an intrusion into the rights of private property. Not long afterward, what he took for evidence of mismanagement and corruption turned him into the Company's most bothersome enemy. A lifelong proponent of religious toleration, he began to hedge noticeably when some English dissenters betrayed signs of sympathy for the French Revolution. He suspended his support of Irish reform to defend absentee landlords—one of the largest of whom was his patron, Rockingham.

But most of his work which justifies continuing study dwelt in one manner or another upon the British constitution, and therein he maintained an impressive consistency for a writer whose vocation was not systematic philosophy but political polemic. The distinction is important. Like most eighteenth-century writers, Burke did not set out to build an all-inclusive philosophical structure, whose parts fitted together harmoniously to make a whole which explained the world. His thought was more empirical, responsive to the issues of the day as they arose, inspired always by the logic of debate, yet still informed by premises and values which were generally consistent with one another and over time as well.

Explicitly or implicitly, nearly all of Burke's political writings and speeches hinged on the supremacy and inviolability of the constitution. Crown and Parliament governed by law and not by whim; their rule was justified because it had lasted, if not forever, at least for very long. That is to say, the constitution had been tested over the centuries, and with untold minute adjustments had been shown to work. It satisfied human needs for order and human aspirations for liberty. Any government so demonstrably successful was not merely good in Burke's eyes, but very nearly sacrosanct. It had proven itself in actual experience, and not on the parchments of metaphysicians. Yet for all its age, it remained vulnerable. To tamper with its organic delicacy was to threaten the work of the ages. From the *Vindication* through the *Reflections,* Burke would place the vital organs of the constitution beyond the reach of political quacks. He was ever alert to events which, however remote, might work some change upon the constitution—and his reverence for it was such that he regarded almost any change as for the worse.

In just this way, Burke wove together his utilitarian and prescriptive arguments. If a set of political arrangements worked tolerably well, that was their justification. If they worked tolerably well over a long period of time, then one could be reasonably confident that they would continue to work well and was therefore denied the right to inquire into their just title. Burke would further bolster political institutions which had attained that status by demanding a cautious evaluation of proposed alternatives. In the *Vindication,* he ridiculed the desirability—even the possibility—of some "natural" utopia. He wanted to know the price of change, assuming all along it would be prohibitively high. More than thirty years later, his tactic was the same, although he could dispose of speculation about immoderate "reform" and simply point to the French Revolution. In 1756, he argued that fundamental change in one public arena would have reverberations throughout the polity. In the 1790s, he could say that the French had made his case for him.

What necessitated the very existence of a government was of course society, and Burke was ever alert to the social ends toward which political instrumentalities must work. Throughout his life he clung firmly to the conviction that government must not only protect social institutions, such as private property, but must also reflect the dominant configurations of social structure. In this respect, Burke carried on—but also substantially deepened—an important trend in British political thought. Going back a century at least to James Harrington, certain British writers had contended that society and government must be conceived as congruent entities, that a people dared not let socioeconomic power and political power rest in different hands. Burke's social analysis of the French Revolution— "The property of France does not govern it"—was the most ambitious undertaking in this vein to his time, but in fact he was only elaborating upon themes he had announced in 1770, when he had bemoaned a shift of influence away from the representatives of property in Parliament toward the court "cabal." Whether he was complaining that taxation of the Americans without their representation was to deprive them of their property, lamenting the political decline of aristocracy, or warning about the deleterious impact of parliamentary reform, the social consequences of political acts were always central to Burke's consciousness.

In the final analysis, Burke was always certain that the constitution and the society it ordered were justified by divine sanction. While his political judgments were often secular in nature, Burke's Christian commitments were ineradicable and pervaded his thought— if often at some rhetorical distance. As a fledgling author, in his parody of Bolingbroke, he had included organized religion among the unassailable institutions. Much of his antipathy for the *philosophes* arose from his mistaken but widely shared assumption that they were atheists. His concept of human nature owed much to the doctrine of original sin. His repeated defenses of an established church revealed the close identification in his mind between religion and government. It was no departure in 1790 when he described individual societies as part of a "great primaeval contract" which connected the creator with all His creation and depicted the state as a divinely willed means for human perfection.

Viewed in this light, it is difficult to find much inconsistency in Burke's response to the great political crises of his time. All of them, from the "discontents" of 1770 to the "Gallic tumults" two

decades later, posed some manner of threat to a constitution which
was hallowed by historical usage, protected by prescription, necessitated and shaped by unalterable social fact, and authored ultimately
by God. He saw the constitution as a subtle balance of various
elements not easily kept in equilibrium. Early in George III's reign,
it appeared that royal influence might upset that balance by ren-
dering Parliament impotent in the face of a "double cabinet." Since
popular liberties were thought to have their chief support in the
House of Commons, Burke cast the threat in terms of a challenge
to freedom. At bottom, however, he was worried about constitutional dislocation and the amassing of undue power in the hands of
executive authority. The same arguments were actually at the root
of his pronouncements on America. For all Burke's talk of an im-
practical war between peoples who shared much in common, he
returned again and again to a concern that deviation by the king's
ministers from long-standing constitutional practices—the refusal
to tax the American colonies in order to raise revenue for England—
would be a precedent the constitution could ill afford to absorb.
His foremost concern was the political health of England, not of
America. His dogged pursuit of Hastings, while proceeding in part
from a desire that justice (as Burke saw it) must be done, stemmed
mainly from his fear that an abuse of authority committed thousands
of miles from home could still taint the domestic constitution.

Burke's reputation as a defender of liberty in the earlier years of
his career was accurate enough, but his efforts were actually undertaken on behalf of preserving the constitution. The consistency
of this motive may perhaps be seen most clearly when one recalls
that he resisted with equal force both the government's harassment
of Wilkes—the premier politician of the *demos* in the 1760s—and
the campaign of radical and democratic reformers to work sweeping
changes in England's system of legislative representation and election. In both cases, vital constitutional principles were at stake and
formed, for Burke, the defining issues. The libertarian rhetoric of
Burke's first ten years or so in the House was therefore a means to
a greater end, the absolute preservation of the constitution—without
which there would be neither liberty nor order nor society. Had
Monsieur Depont grasped this basic reality, he would never have
invited Burke to deliver an endorsement of events in France during
1789. How could Burke possibly, consistent with his principles,
approve the nationalization and sale of church property or the process

by which a constitution would be instantly concocted by a batch of petty lawyers and rustic curates?

Burke was consistent as well in his evaluation of political thought and behavior. From the very outset, and scarcely without faltering, he would ask first of all about consequences. Appeals to justice and other "higher" principles came rarely from his pen. The case, made so often in recent years by approving commentators on Burke, that he was part of the classical natural law school fails not so much of implausibility as from extremely sparse and scattered evidence in his writings. The most that can be said is that if Burke was indeed a part of that ancient intellectual tradition, then he employed its conceptual apparatus and its vocabulary far less than any of his predecessors. All in all, it makes more sense to see Burke as a man who wished to know how things were going to work, what sorts of changes a proposal would entail, whether something was feasible, what one had to accept and what one had to reject to go along with a given idea. Like so many men in the eighteenth century, his highest criterion for public acts was social utility, which for all intents and purposes he equated with preservation of the English constitution.

Another way to approach this matter of Burke's consistency is to say that he was consistently conservative. Burke's constitutional thought hinged upon the Revolution Settlement of 1688–89. When he considered it, the descriptive and the normative categories of his mind became virtually interchangeable. Difficulties arose not because the Settlement was in any way inadequate, but rather because men foolishly allowed some drift from the course it had marked out. Burke resisted change for the sake of the Revolution Settlement and occasionally advocated change in the hope of restoring its original intent. Although in fact he shared much ground with the *philosophes* he so warmly castigated, here was a vital difference between them. Most *philosophes,* while eschewing utopianism, would marshal human resources in the cause of constant improvement, in gradually but hopefully laying the groundwork for a better future. For Burke, the future lay in the past; he would guard against its erosion, labor incessantly to renew it, meet all attempts to "interpret" or "modernize" it with the coldest suspicion.

Such attitudes are probably as serviceable a definition of conservatism as one may find. Like most "isms," it is a sadly battered word, one which did not exist in Burke's own age but which has since become a political label elastic enough to fit a variety of postures—some of them mutually contradictory. It has long since been routine to assume that Burke was father to them all, if for no other reason than that many learned authors have pronounced that he was the fountainhead of modern conservatism. In fact, the search for authentic disciples can be frustrating.

It is sometimes said that, among English conservatives, quoting Burke has long been a substitute for thought. The truth, as usual, is less droll and more instructive. Nineteenth-century conservatives and representatives of the social elite whose dominance Burke sought to maintain refused to follow his policy of unbending resistance, perhaps because they were temperamentally more flexible, or perhaps because they realized that events had rendered Burke's counsel obsolete. In any event, first in 1832 and then again in 1867, major reform of parliamentary representation and election came at the behest of aristocratic leaders. The growing northern regions of England won increased share of seats in the Commons while the franchise broadened down into newer middle-class strata and even into modestly propertied elements. It was reform of exactly the sort which Burke had vociferously opposed during the 1780s.

It may of course be argued that, two generations after his own time, Burke might have changed his views to accord with altered conditions. Yet it must still be noted that his worst blind spot was just there—in the inability to build adaptive mechanisms into his political thought. It was not that he failed to see into the nineteenth century, at least part of the way, for he was sensitive to the threat embodied in what he called the "moneyed interest." If his description of the French Revolution was not without flaws, still he anticipated the lurking conflict between the middle classes and the landed classes, the possibility of temporary alliance between the urban bourgeoisie and the masses, and the ultimate rupture of that alliance. In every respect, he was sketching out the political struggles of England and the Continent as well for the next sixty years. The problem was that Burke had no means of dealing with all this beyond a furious commitment to a social and political order which were doomed—for reasons of which he was ignorant. The constitution, in his eyes, could always adapt to shifting *political* circumstances— such as the ominous enhancement of court influence—by going back to the principles of the Revolution Settlement. But the very notion of fundamental social change which would render old political arrangements anachronistic simply left Burke at a loss.

His alleged heirs knew better. They realized that they could mix a measure of concession with a huge dose of continuity, that constitutional change might perpetuate most of the stratified aristocratic society and the politics of deference by palliating strategically located opponents. The first two reform acts of the nineteenth century were not so much a surrender as a strategic withdrawal which gave up far less ground than may have been apparent. They were shrewd compromises fully worthy of prudent and subtle politicians of the sort Burke wished to have in power; but they were also compromises which Burke rigidly rejected in his own lifetime. It was much the same on the Continent, where conservative statesmen in France— and to a greater degree in Germany and Austria-Hungary—made partial peace with the legatees of the French Revolution and absorbed liberal institutions while retaining the substance of their own predominance well into the nineteenth century.

Thus, while conservatives after Burke cited his stately prose incessantly—with or without a good excuse—they did not, and could not, very often imitate his political behavior. Far from being the father of modern conservatism, Burke was rather more like the last voice of a dying age, notable chiefly for the eloquence and passion with which he championed a politics which events would soon render antique. Only if one conceives of Burke's politics as tactic rather than as program do modern analogues appear. The so-called strict constructionist interpretation of the American constitution comes immediately to mind. This approach would, at least in theory, take that eighteenth-century document as literally as possible and exceed its mandates only with the very greatest reluctance. This is a conservatism Burke might well have comprehended, whatever he thought of the constitution itself.

However this may be, Burke still continues to provide a wealth of political and moral wisdom from which persons of all persuasions may benefit. No one has written more informatively upon the profound consequentiality of public acts, upon the need to examine all the implications of political decisions, upon the necessity of accompanying the question, "Is this the *right* thing to do?" with the question, "Is this a *good* thing to do?" However great the need may be for change in any society at any time, some measure of stability is always equally vital, a subject on which Burke was unsurpassed in acuity. He was sensitive to the desire for justice, but even more to that for freedom, which he knew required order above all. Finally, whether men wish it or not, and defy it as they may, the past will always have its due from them. Burke understood this truth, and tried to find ways to help men to accommodate to it. His efforts remain eminently worthy of reflection.

Notes and References

Chapter One

1. Letter of 24 December 1747, in Thomas W. Copeland, gen. ed., *The Correspondence of Edmund Burke* (Cambridge and Chicago, 1958–70), 1:101. (Hereinafter cited as *Correspondence.*)

2. H. V. F. Somerset, ed., *A Note-Book of Edmund Burke* (Cambridge: Cambridge University Press, 1957), p. 21.

3. James T. Boulton has prepared an excellent critical edition of the *Enquiry* with an extensive introduction. I have used the version issued by the University of Notre Dame Press (Notre Dame and London, 1968). See here especially pp. xv–xxii and lxxxi–cxxvii.

4. In 1757, Will Burke published *An Account of the European Settlements in America,* upon which Edmund also did substantial work.

5. Since articles in the *Annual Register* were not signed, and since the extent of Burke's involvement in the journal after the mid-1760s is debatable, it seems risky to chart his intellectual growth by relying heavily upon pieces in the *Register.* For details on this whole subject, see Thomas W. Copeland, *Our Eminent Friend Edmund Burke* (New Haven, 1949), pp. 92–145.

6. To follow the development of Burke's sophistication in the workings of everyday politics, see especially his latters to Charles O'Hara, an old and politically knowledgeable Irish friend, in *Correspondence,* I.

7. Letter of 11 July 1765, ibid., p. 211.

8. Letter of 11 December 1767, ibid., p. 340.

9. Quoted in Isaac Kramnick, ed., *Edmund Burke* (Englewood Cliffs, N.J., 1974), p. 94.

10. On the finances of the Burke family, see Copeland, *Our Eminent Friend,* pp. 41–70, and Dixon Wector, *Edmund Burke and His Kinsmen* (Boulder: University of Colorado, 1939).

11. Letter of November 1772, in *Correspondence,* 2:377.

12. The remark goes through several versions in the different editions of Boswell's *Life.* See Thomas W. Copeland, "Johnson and Burke," in Anne Whiteman et al., *Statesmen, Scholars and Merchants: Essays in Eighteenth-Century History Presented to Dame Lucy Sutherland* (Oxford: Clarendon Press, 1973), pp. 300–302.

Chapter Two

1. *The Works of the Right Honorable Edmund Burke* (Boston, 1904), 3:377.
2. See Donald Cross Bryant, *Edmund Burke and His Literary Friends* (St. Louis, 1939).
3. Somerset, ed., *A Note-Book*, p. 71.
4. *Works*, 1:5.
5. Ibid., pp. 24–25.
6. Ibid., p. 49.
7. Ibid., p. 55.
8. Ibid., p. 59.
9. Ibid., p. 60.
10. Ibid., pp. 57, 62, 65.
11. Ibid., p. 6.
12. Somerset, ed., *A Note-Book*, p. 90.
13. *Works*, 1:9.
14. Ibid., p. 13.
15. Boulton ed., *Enquiry*, pp. xv–xxii.
16. *Works*, 1:110–11.
17. Ibid., pp. lxxxi–cxxvii.
18. *Works*, 7:268.
19. Ibid., p. 362.
20. Ibid., p. 409.
21. Ibid., p. 467.
22. *Works*, 1:443.
23. *Works*, 3:276.
24. Ibid., p. 331.
25. *Works*, 2:449–50.
26. *Works*, 3:361.
27. See the extremely persuasive analysis in Paul Fussell, *The Rhetorical World of Augustan Humanism: Ethics and Imagery from Swift to Burke* (Oxford, 1965).
28. Sigmund Freud, *Civilization and Its Discontents* (New York: Norton, 1962), trans. James Strachey, p. 58.
29. See the provocative, but often infuriatingly speculative, arguments in Isaac Kramnick, *The Rage of Edmund Burke: Portrait of An Ambivalent Conservative* (New York, 1977).
30. *Works*, 5:199.
31. Speech of 14 May 1781, in *The Speeches of the Right Honourable Edmund Burke* (London, 1816), II, 257.
32. Speech of 15 June 1781, in *Works*, VII, 134.
33. *Works*, 3:291.
34. Ibid., p. 299.

35. *Works,* 1:457–58.
36. Especially by Fussell, *The Rhetorical World of Augustan Humanism.*
37. *Works,* 2:229.
38. *Works,* 3:287.
39. Ibid., p. 434.
40. Ibid., p. 438.
41. *Works,* 7:97.
42. Ibid., p. 73.

Chapter Three

1. On the Wilkes affair, see George Rudé, *Wilkes and Liberty: A Social Study of 1763 to 1774* (Oxford: Oxford University Press, 1962).
2. *Thoughts,* in *Works,* 1:437.
3. Ibid., p. 444.
4. Ibid., p. 446.
5. Ibid., p. 458.
6. Ibid., p. 459.
7. Ibid., pp. 473–74.
8. Ibid., p. 472.
9. Ibid., p. 492.
10. Ibid., p. 499.
11. Ibid., p. 507.
12. Ibid., p. 515–16.
13. Ibid., p. 520.
14. Ibid., p. 521.
15. Ibid., p. 523.
16. Ibid., p. 526.
17. *Observations,* in *Works,* 7:271.
18. Ibid., p. 419.
19. *Thoughts,* in *Works,* 1:527.
20. Ibid., p. 529.
21. Ibid., p. 530.
22. Ibid., p. 530–31.
23. Ibid., p. 535.
24. Ibid., p. 520.
25. Ibid., p. 537.
26. Much of the debate over this and other issues from the period may be followed in Herbert Butterfield, *George III and the Historians* (New York, rev. ed., 1959).
27. Speech of 7 March 1771, in *Works,* 7:107–22.
28. Speech of 8 May 1780, in ibid., pp. 71–87; *Speech on American Taxation,* in *Works,* 2:37; speech of 14 June 1784, in ibid., 537–76; address to the king in January 1777, in *Works,* 6:173.

29. Speech of 11 February 1780, in *Works*, 2:267.

30. Ibid., pp. 280–81.

31. Speech of 7 February 1771, in *Works*, 7:61–67.

32. *Observations*, in *Works*, 1:371.

33. Speech of 15 June 1781, in *Works*, 7:134.

34. In Burke's *Works*, this is usually identified as the Speech of 7 May 1782; however, R. R. Palmer has made a plausible case that it was actually prepared for delivery in June of 1784. See *The Age of the Democratic Revolution* (Princeton: Princeton University Press, 1:313–14n. For the sake of convenience in citation, however, I will retain the traditional dating—since to change would make consultation of the source troublesome.

35. Speech of 7 May 1782, in *Works*, 7:101, 102, 103.

36. Ibid., p. 104.

37. Ibid., p. 93.

38. Ibid., p. 94.

39. Harvey C. Mansfield, Jr., *Statesmanship and Party Government: A Study of Burke and Bolingbroke* (Chicago and London, 1965), p. 221.

40. It is so argued in ibid.

41. Speech of 7 May 1782, in *Works*, 7:94.

42. Ibid., p. 95.

43. Ibid.

44. See Carl B. Cone, *Burke and the Nature of Politics*, Volume 1: *The Age of the American Revolution* (Lexington, Ky., 1956), pp. 162–65; Paul Lucas, "On Edmund Burke's Doctrine of Prescription; or, An Appeal from the New to the Old Lawyers," *Historical Journal* 11, no. 1 (1968):35–63.

45. Speech of 3 November 1774, in *Works*, 2:89–98.

46. *Speech Relative to his Parliamentary Conduct*, in *Works*, 2:370–71.

47. Speech of 6 February 1772, in *Works*, 7:12–13.

48. Ibid., p. 8.

49. Speech of 17 February 1772, in *Works*, 7:139.

50. Speech of 6 February 1772, in *Works*, 7:10.

51. Speech of 17 March 1773, in *Works*, 7:25.

52. Ibid., p. 37.

53. Ibid.

54. "Letter to William Smith, Esq., on the Subject of Catholic Emancipation," 29 January 1795, in *Works*, 6:361–73; see also the "Letter to Richard Burke, Esq., on Pro Protestant Ascendency in Ireland," 1793, in *Works*, 6:385–412.

55. *Speech Relative to his Parliamentary Conduct*, in *Works*, 2:421.

56. Ibid., p. 405.

57. Ibid., p. 418.

58. See, among many examples, the *Letter to the Sheriffs of Bristol* (1777), in *Works*, 2:228–29; "A Letter to the Chairman of the Buckinghamshire

Meeting, held at Aylesbury, April 13, 1780, on the Subject of Parliamentary Reform," in *Works*, 6:294.

Chapter Four

1. Copeland, "Johnson and Burke," pp.. 299–300.
2. *Letter to the Sheriffs of Bristol*, in *Works*, 2:223.
3. *Speech on American Taxation*, in *Works*, 2:77.
4. Ibid., pp. 75–76.
5. Ibid., p. 76.
6. *Letter to the Sheriffs of Bristol*, in *Works*, 2:227.
7. *Speech on American Taxation*, in *Works*, 2:75.
8. *Speech on Conciliation with America*, in *Works*, 2:117.
9. *Letter to the Sheriffs of Bristol*, in *Works*, 2:223–24.
10. *Speech on American Taxation*, in *Works*, 2:77.
11. *Speech on Conciliation with America*, in *Works*, 2:146–53.
12. *Observations*, in *Works*, 1:372–76.
13. *Speech on Conciliation with America*, in *Works*, 2:170.
14. *Letter to the Sheriffs of Bristol*, in *Works*, 2:193.
15. *Speech on American Taxation*, in *Works*, 2:73.
16. On this subject, see Paul Langford, "The Rockingham Whigs and America, 1767–1773," in Whiteman et al., *Statesmen, Scholars and Merchants*, pp. 135–52.
17. *Speech on American Taxation*, in *Works*, 2:73.
18. Ibid., pp. 73–74.
19. *Speech on Conciliation with America*, in *Works*, 2:181–82.
20. *Letter to the Sheriffs of Bristol*, in *Works*, 2:203.
21. Ibid., p. 206.
22. "Address to the British Colonists in North America," in *Works*, 6:183–96.
23. *Speech on Fox's East India Bill*, in *Works*, 2:436.
24. Ibid.
25. First speech before the House of Lords in the trial of Warren Hastings, in *Works*, 9:342.
26. Ibid., p. 332. On the Hastings case in general, I am indebted to P. J. Marshall, *The Impeachment of Warren Hastings* (Oxford, 1965).
27. *Tract on the Popery Laws*, in *Works*, 6:320–21.
28. Ibid., p. 322.
29. Ibid., p. 334.
30. Ibid., pp. 340–41.
31. "Two Letters to Gentlemen in the City of Bristol," 1778, in *Works*, 2:249–64.
32. *Speech on Conciliation with America*, in *Works*, 2:147.
33. *First Letter to Sir Hercules Langrishe*, in *Works*, 4:271.

34. "A Letter on the Affairs of Ireland," 1797, in *Works*, 6:420–21.
35. Ibid., p. 421.
36. "A Letter to Sir Charles Bingham," 30 October 1773, in *Works*, 6:125.
37. Thomas H. D. Mahoney, *Edmund Burke and Ireland* (Cambridge, Mass., 1960), is a helpful guide to this general subject.
38. First speech in the Hastings trial, in *Works*, 9:398.
39. Ibid., 398–99.

Chapter Five

1. Letter of 9 August 1789, in *Correspondence*, 6:10.
2. Letter of 27 September 1789, in ibid., pp. 25–26.
3. Letter of 12 November 1789, in ibid., p. 36.
4. *Reflections*, in *Works*, 3:243–44.
5. Speech of 9 February 1790, in *Works*, 3:223.
6. See the analysis of style in James T. Boulton, *The Language of Politics in the Age of Wilkes and Burke* (London and Toronto, 1963), pp. 97–133.
7. *Reflections*, in *Works*, 3:299–300.
8. Ibid., p. 297.
9. Ibid., p. 241.
10. Ibid., p. 309.
11. Ibid., p. 310.
12. Ibid., p. 309.
13. Ibid., p. 310.
14. *Letter to the Sheriffs of Bristol*, in *Works*, 2:229.
15. *Reflections*, in *Works*, 3:312.
16. Ibid., p. 283, 286.
17. Ibid., pp. 287–88.
18. Ibid., p. 291.
19. Ibid., p. 295.
20. Ibid., p. 296.
21. Ibid., p. 331.
22. Ibid.
23. Ibid.
24. Ibid.
25. Ibid., p. 333.
26. Ibid., p. 334.
27. Letter of 20 February 1790, in *Correspondence*, VI, 91.
28. *Reflections*, in *Works*, 3:337.
29. Ibid., pp. 345–46.
30. Ibid., p. 346.

31. See, for example, George V. Taylor, "Non-Capitalist Wealth and the Origins of the French Revolution," *American Historical Review* 72 (January 1967):469–96.

32. *Reflections*, in *Works*, 3:377.

33. Ibid., p. 381.

34. Ibid., pp. 367–68.

35. Ibid., pp. 362–63.

36. Ibid., p. 354.

37. Ibid., p. 394.

38. Ibid., p. 298.

39. Ibid., p. 486.

40. Ibid., p. 489.

41. Ibid., p. 491.

42. Letter of ca. 6 August 1793, in *Correspondence*, 7:389.

43. *Reflections*, in *Works*, 3:528–31.

44. Speech of 11 April 1794, in *Speeches*, 4:166.

45. Letter of ca. 6 August 1793, in *Correspondence*, 7:389–90.

46. *Thoughts on French Affairs*, in *Works*, 4:350.

47. *Reflections*, in *Works*, 3:436–38.

48. Speech of 11 April 1794, in *Speeches*, 4:165–66.

49. *Reflections*, in *Works*, 3:335.

50. Ibid., p. 444.

51. Speech of 4 May 1772, in *Speeches*, 1:126.

52. *Reflections*, in *Works*, 3:445.

53. Ibid., p. 277.

54. *Thoughts and Details on Scarcity*, in *Works*, 5:136.

55. Ibid., p. 157.

56. *Reflections*, in *Works*, 3:445.

57. Ibid.

58. *Thoughts and Details on Scarcity*, in *Works*, 5:133–34.

59. Letter of November 1777, in *Correspondence*, 3:402–4.

60. Letter of January 1777, in *Works*, 6:164.

61. Speech of 14 May 1781, in *Speeches*, 2:257–58.

62. Speech of 11 February 1780, in *Works*, 2:329.

63. *Reflections*, in *Works*, 3:447.

64. Ibid., p. 274.

65. Ibid., p. 275.

66. Ibid., p. 272.

67. Ibid., p. 271.

68. Letter of 26 February 1790, in *Correspondence*, VI, 95.

69. Ibid., p. 94.

70. *Reflections*, in *Works*, 3:361.

71. Ibid., p. 359.

72. Ibid., p. 457.
73. Ibid., p. 481.
74. *Letters on a Regicide Peace,* in *Works,* 5:361.
75. Speech of 13 December 1793, in *Speeches,* 4:76.
76. *Reflections,* in *Works,* 3:557–58.
77. Ibid., p. 351.
78. Ibid., pp. 412–13.
79. Ibid., p. 416.
80. Ibid., p. 288.
81. Ibid., pp. 433–34.

Chapter Six

1. *Letter to a Member of the French National Assembly,* in *Works,* 4:4–5.
2. Ibid., p. 52.
3. See *Thoughts on French Affairs,* in *Works,* 4:313–77.
4. Letter of ca. 6 August 1793, in *Correspondence,* 7:387–90; speech of 11 April 1794, in *Speeches,* 4:167.
5. *Three Letters on a Regicide Peace,* in *Works,* 5:309–10.
6. *Thoughts on French Affairs,* in *Works,* 4:319.
7. *Remarks on the Policy of the Allies,* in *Works,* 4:449; *Three Letters on a Regicide Peace,* in *Works,* 5:250.
8. *Remarks on the Policy of the Allies,* in *Works,* 4:427–29.
9. See the letter to William Smith, in *Works* 6:361–73; "Second Letter to Sir Hercules Langrishe," in *Works,* 6:375–84; letter to Richard Burke, in *Works,* 6:385–412.
10. Carl B. Cone, *Burke and the Nature of Politics,* Vol. 2: *The Age of the French Revolution* (Lexington, Ky., 1962), pp. 341–42.
11. Edmund Burke and Thomas Paine, *Reflections on the Revolution in France & The Rights of Man* (New York: Doubleday, 1961), p. 278.
12. Ibid., p. 288.
13. In the *Reflections,* Burke wrote: "Abstractedly speaking, government, as well as liberty, is good; yet could I, in common sense, ten years ago, have felicitated France on her enjoyment of a government (for she then had a government) without enquiry what the nature of that government was, or how it was administered?" (ibid., p. 19). In *The Rights of Man,* Paine wrote: "But Mr. Burke appears to have no idea of principles, when he is contemplating governments. 'Ten Years ago,' says he, 'I could have felicitated France on her having a government, without inquiring what the nature of that government was, or how it was administered.' Is this the language of a rational man? . . . ." (ibid., p. 285).
14. Ibid., p. 305.
15. Letter of 21 November 1791, in *Correspondence,* VI, 451.
16. *Appeal,* in *Works,* 4:207.

17. Ibid., p. 165.
18. Ibid., p. 166.
19. Ibid., p. 174.
20. Ibid., p. 175.
21. Ibid., p. 176.
22. Ibid., p. 202.
23. *Observations on the Conduct of the Minority*, in *Works*, 5:7–63.
24. *Three Letters on a Regicide Peace*, in *Works*, 5:285.
25. *Fourth Letter on a Regicide Peace*, in *Works*, 6:107.
26. Letter of 12 May 1797, in *Correspondence*, 9:340.
27. *A Letter to a Noble Lord*, in *Works*, 5:187.
28. Ibid., p. 193.
29. Ibid., p. 201.
30. Ibid., p. 209.
31. Ibid., p. 211.
32. Ibid., p. 213.

Selected Bibliography

PRIMARY SOURCES

The Correspondence of Edmund Burke. Thomas W. Copeland, gen. ed. 10 vols. Cambridge: Cambridge University Press, and Chicago: University of Chicago Press, 1958–70.

The Speeches of the Right Honourable Edmund Burke. 4 vols. London: Longman, Hurst, Rees, Orme, and Brown, 1816.

The Works of the Right Honorable Edmund Burke. 12 vols. Boston: Little, Brown, and Co., 1904. Professor Paul Langford, of Oxford University, is heading the project to issue a scholarly edition of Burke's works in the course of the 1980s.

N.B. No edition of Burke's works includes his contributions to the *Annual Register*, since none of the articles therein was signed and authorship in many cases is in doubt. On this subject, see the reference in note 5, Chapter 1.

SECONDARY SOURCES

The following is by no means an exhaustive bibliography of Burke studies, but is intended rather to indicate the most useful studies consulted in the preparation of this book and to serve as well as a guide to further inquiry.

Barrington, Donal. "Edmund Burke as an Economist." *Economica*, new series, 21 (1954):252–58. A brief look at Burke's sketchily expressed economic thought, and its relation to the ideas associated with Adam Smith.

Bate, W. J., ed. *Edmund Burke: Selected Works.* New York: Modern Library, 1960. Notable mainly for the introduction (pp. 3–39), which is a thoughtful review of Burke's life and mind.

Baumann, Arthur A. *Burke: The Founder of Conservatism.* London: Eyre and Spottiswoode, 1929. An unscholarly but amusing defense of

Burke as a "reactionary," informative as to the lengths commentators will go to bring Burke "up to date."

Bevan, Ruth A. *Marx and Burke: A Revisionist View.* La Salle, Ill.: Open Court, 1973. Notes the obvious differences and certain similarities in their thought, but fails to put adequate stress on parallels in social preoccupations.

Bickel, Alexander M. *The Morality of Consent.* New Haven: Yale University Press, 1975. A brief but provocative subchapter attempts, not very convincingly, to absorb Burke into the liberal tradition.

Bisset, Robert. *The Life of Edmund Burke.* London: George Cawthorn, 1798. The first attempt at biography, a year after Burke's death; some interesting anecdotes, but not as useful as the larger work by Prior.

Boorstin, Daniel J. *The Mysterious Science of the Law.* Cambridge, Mass.: Harvard University Press, 1941. The final chapter is an examination of Burke's views on prescription and the constitution in historical perspective.

Boulton, James T. *Arbitrary Power: An Eighteenth-Century Obsession.* Nottingham: University of Nottingham, n.d. One of Burke's favorite subjects; there are here repeated references to his views but little analysis of them.

—————. "Burke's *Letter to a Noble Lord:* Apologia and Manifesto." *Burke Newsletter* 8 (1967):695–701. Argues that Burke attempted to celebrate aristocracy and the "new man" in politics at the same time.

—————. *The Language of Politics in the Age of Wilkes and Burke.* London: Routledge and Kegan Paul, and Toronto: University of Toronto Press, 1963. An important chapter on rhetorical strategies in the *Reflections.*

—————, ed. *A Philosophical Enquiry into the Origin of Our Ideas of the Sublime and Beautiful.* Notre Dame and London: University of Notre Dame Press, 1968. Especially useful historical and analytical introduction to Burke's treatise on aesthetics.

Brewer, John. "The Misfortunes of Lord Bute: A Case Study in Eighteenth-Century Political Argument and Public Opinion." *Historical Journal* 16 (1973):3–43.

—————. "Party and Double Cabinet: Two Facets of Burke's Thoughts." *Historical Journal* 14 (1971):479–501.

—————. "Rockingham, Burke, and Whig Political Argument." *Historical Journal* 18 (1975):188–201. This and the preceding articles by the same author attempt to treat Burke's ideas between 1770 and 1782 less as the development of political philosophy than as an effort to employ a politically effective argument in the circumstances and vocabulary of the eighteenth-century Parliament. Brewer strikes some effective blows against the notion of Burke as a "natural law" thinker.

Bryant, Donald C. *Edmund Burke and His Literary Friends.* Washington University Studies, new series, Language and Literature, no. 9. St. Louis: Washington University Press, 1939. Details on Burke's contacts with the London literary world, though little of value on the obscure decade of the 1750s.

Butterfield, Herbert. *George III and the Historians.* New York: Macmillan, revised edition, 1959. Still the best historiographical review of the major issues in the monarch's reign.

Cobban, Alfred. *Edmund Burke and the Revolt against the Eighteenth Century: A Study of the Political and Social Thinking of Burke, Wordsworth, Coleridge, and Southey.* London: Macmillan, 1929. The fullest statement of Burke as the herald of Romanticism, rejecting the central values of his century; Cobban withdrew somewhat from this exposed position in a 1961 edition of the book published in New York by Barnes and Noble.

Cone, Carl B. *Burke and the Nature of Politics.* 2 vols. Lexington: University of Kentucky Press, 1957–64. The first volume deals with Burke through the age of the American Revolution, the second to the end of his life. The standard political biography, though not all that might be desired as a study of Burke's intellectual life. Based upon extensive work in unpublished papers.

Copeland, Thomas W. "Johnson and Burke." In Anne Whiteman, J. S. Bromley, and P. G. M. Dickson, eds. *Statesmen, Scholars and Merchants: Essays in Eighteenth-Century History presented to Dame Lucy Sutherland.* Oxford: Clarendon Press, 1973, pp. 289–303. An interesting study of the relations between the two friends, who were often at odds over various public questions, based largely upon remarks from various editions from Boswell's *Life.*

———. *Our Eminent Friend Edmund Burke.* New Haven: Yale University Press, 1949. Six separate but by no means disconnected essays on often neglected aspects of Burke's life and career, including his journalistic career and the various forms of public abuse to which he was subject.

Courtney, C. P. "Edmund Burke and the Enlightenment." In Anne Whiteman et al. *Statesmen, Scholars and Merchants: Essays in Eighteenth-Century History presented to Dame Lucy Sutherland.* Oxford, Clarendon Press, 1973, pp. 304–22. An insightful revision of Cobban's thesis, pointing out Burke's affinities with Montesquieu and the earlier generation of the Enlightenment.

———. *Montesquieu and Burke.* Oxford: Basil Blackwell, 1963. An important comparative study demonstrating Montesquieu's influence upon Burke.

Deane, Seamus F. "Burke and the French *Philosophes.*" *Studies in Burke and His Time* 10 (1968–69):113–37. Sees Burke favorable to Montesquieu but hostile to Voltaire and Rousseau; some interesting remarks on the imagery in Burke's writings.

Derry, John W. *The Regency Crisis and the Whigs, 1788–9.* Cambridge: Cambridge University Press, 1963. Includes material on Burke's role during this brief glimmer of Whig hope.

Dinwiddy, J. R. "Utility and Natural Law in Burke's Thought: A Reconsideration." *Studies in Burke and His Time* 16 (1974–75):105–28. Emphasizes the role of utility in Burke's thought, especially when it came to the question of property rights.

Dreyer, Frederick. "Edmund Burke: The Philosopher in Action." *Studies in Burke and His Time* 15 (1973–74):121–42. Argues against the natural law interpretation.

Einaudi, Mario. "The British Background of Burke's Political Philosophy." *Political Science Quarterly* 49 (1934):576–98. Surveys some of the seventeenth- and eighteenth-century thinkers who anticipated Burke and explored similar problems.

Fennessy, R. R. *Burke, Paine and the Rights of Man: A Difference of Political Opinion.* The Hague: Martinus Nijhoff, 1963. Analyzes the debate between Burke and Paine only to conclude that they were not debating at all but simply using each other's works as pretexts for expressing their own preconceived views.

Fitzgerald, John J. "The Logical Style of Burke's Thoughts on the Cause of the Present Discontents." *Burke Newsletter* 7 (1965):465–78. Notes elements of both simplicity and complexity in the logical structure of the pamphlet.

Fussell, Paul. *The Rhetorical World of Augustan Humanism: Ethics and Imagery from Swift to Burke.* Oxford: Clarendon Press, 1965. The best study of Burke as writer, firmly connecting him with an important tradition.

Ganzin, Michel. *La pensée politique d'Edmund Burke.* Paris: Librairie Générale de Droit et de Jurisprudence, 1972. A lengthy and wholly too abstract attempt at synthesis which suffers from a failure to root Burke in his political career and an apparent ignorance of the materials in the *Correspondence.*

Graubard, Stephen R. *Burke, Disraeli, and Churchill: The Politics of Perseverance.* Cambridge, Mass.: Harvard University Press, 1961. Locates Burke at the source of a British tradition of rather utilitarian conservatism.

Hart, Jeffrey. "Burke and Radical Freedom." *Review of Politics* 29 (1967):221–38. A sympathetic defense of Burke's attack on abstract definitions of freedom from an avowedly conservative point of view.

Hill, B. W. "Fox and Burke: The Whig Party and the question of principles, 1784–1789." *English Historical Review* 89 (1974):3–24. Argues plausibly that the split in the Whig party was bound to come in any event, and that the French revolution merely provided the issue for it.

Hoffmann, R. J. S. *Edmund Burke: New York Agent.* Philadelphia: The American Philosophical Society, 1956. A detailed study of Burke's period representing the interest of the state of New York.

————. *The Marquis: A Study of Lord Rockingham, 1730–1782.* New York: Fordham University Press, 1973. A carefully researched biography of Burke's most important patron.

————, and **Levack, Paul,** eds. *Burke's Politics: Selected Writings and Speeches.* New York: Alfred A. Knopf, 1959. The introduction is one of the earliest statements of the natural law interpretation.

Joy, Neill R. "Burke's *Speech on Conciliation with the Colonies*: Epic Prophecy and Satire." *Studies in Burke and His Time* 9 (1967):753–72. Shows the strong neo-classical influences upon Burke's oratorical style, for which the author finds sources especially in Pope and Dryden.

Kirk, Russell. *The Conservative Mind from Burke to Santayana.* Chicago: Henry Regnery Company, 1953. Probably the most significant attempt of American "neo-conservatives" of the 1950s to establish Burke as their spiritual forefather and the fountainhead of modern conservative thought.

Kramnick, Isaac, ed. *Edmund Burke.* Englewood Cliffs, N.J.: Prentice-Hall, "Great Lives Observed," 1974. A sometimes handy collection of edited short pieces by and about Burke.

————. *The Rage of Edmund Burke: Portrait of An Ambivalent Conservative.* New York: Basic Books, 1977. A controversial, provocative, and ultimately unsatisfying attempt at a psychoanalytical explanation of Burke.

————. "Skepticism in English Political Thought: From Temple to Burke." *Studies in Burke and His Time* 12 (1970):627–60. Finds Burke's conservatism in his skeptical response to novelty and metaphysics; isolates an interesting tradition in British thought.

Langford, Paul. "The Rockingham Whigs and America, 1767–1773." In Anne Whiteman et al. *Statesmen, Scholars and Merchants: Essays in Eighteenth-Century History presented to Dame Lucy Sutherland.* Oxford: Clarendon Press, 1973, pp. 135–52. Demonstrates that the Rockinghams were by no means in the forefront for American independence and underscores the numerous conservative features of their policy.

Laski, Harold J. *Political Thought in England from Locke to Bentham.* New York: Henry Holt and Co., and London: Williams and Norgate,

1920. The long chapter on Burke is a surprisingly sympathetic reading from the Fabian left.

Love, Walter D. "Burke's Transition from a Literary to a Political Career." *Burke Newsletter* 6 (1964–65):376–90. Stresses the concern over Irish problems as the primary motive for Burke's move toward political involvement.

————. "Edmund Burke's Idea of the Body Corporate: A Study in Imagery." *Review of Politics* 27 (1965):184–97. Argues that Burke's relatively static conception of society as the "body corporate" runs counter to the implicitly evolutionary aspects of an "organic" view of society.

Lucas, Paul. "On Edmund Burke's Doctrine of Prescription; or, An Appeal from the New to the Old Lawyers." *Historical Journal* 11 (1968):35–63. A brilliant analysis of the importance of prescription in Burke's thought and the absence of its debt to the natural law tradition.

MacCunn, John. *The Political Philosophy of Burke*. London: Edward Arnold, 1913. A clear-headed and by no means outdated study of Burke's political writings, still useful as an introduction.

MacPherson, C. B. "Edmund Burke." *Transactions of the Royal Society of Canada,* series 3, 53 (1959):19–26. A brief but extremely suggestive Marxist analysis of Burke's social and economic views.

————. "Edmund Burke and the New Conservatism." *Science and Society* 22 (1958):231–39. A review essay which raises some interesting questions about the revival of conservative interest in Burke during the 1950s.

Magnus, Philip. *Edmund Burke: A Life.* London: John Murray, 1939. Though in many respects superseded by Cone, still the most readable biography of Burke.

Mahoney, Thomas H. D. *Edmund Burke and Ireland.* Cambridge: Harvard University Press, 1960. A detailed account of Burke's dealing with and hope for his native country.

Mansfield, Harvey C., Jr. *Statesmanship and Party Government: A Study of Burke and Bolingbroke.* Chicago and London: University of Chicago Press, 1965. Although concentrating heavily upon Burke's *Thoughts*, the author proposes a number of suggestions which are useful for the interpretation of Burke's entire corpus.

Marshall, P. J. *The Impeachment of Warren Hastings.* Oxford: Oxford University Press, 1965. A model of scholarly investigation and dispassion which not only casts light upon the degree of Hastings' culpability but also thoroughly ventilates Burke's motives and conduct during the case.

Mitchell, L. G. *Charles James Fox and the Disintegration of the Whig Party, 1782–1794.* Oxford: Oxford University Press, 1971. A valuable study of the Whigs and of the relations between Burke and Fox, especially during the critical years of the French revolution.

Morley, John. *Burke.* New York: J. W. Lovell, 1884. The best nineteenth-century biography, sympathetic enough to be insightful, but distanced still by a strong dash of mid-Victorian liberalism.

O'Brien, Conor Cruise, ed. *Reflections on the Revolution in France.* Baltimore: Penguin Books, 1969. Useful for the introduction (pp. 9–76), where O'Brien argues that while Burke's position was a conservative and counterrevolutionary one with respect to France, it was exactly the opposite with respect to Ireland.

O'Gorman, Frank. *Edmund Burke: His Political Philosophy.* Bloomington and London: Indiana University Press, 1973. A helpful brief study, strong on the importance of Burke's commitment to the rights of property.

Oliver, Barbara C. "Edmund Burke's 'Enquiry' and the Baroque Theory of the Passions." *Studies in Burke and His Time* 12 (1970):1661–76. Traces the origins of certain of Burke's aesthetic and psychological ideas.

Osborn, Annie Marion. *Rousseau and Burke: A Study of the Idea of Liberty in Eighteenth-Century Political Thought.* New York: Russell and Russell, 1964. First published in 1940, this study concentrates on the rather obvious differences between the two men.

Parkin, Charles. *The Moral Basis of Burke's Political Thought.* Cambridge: Cambridge University Press, 1956. Emphasizes the natural law, and more particularly, the Christian basis of Burke's ideas.

Pocock, J. G. A. "Burke and the Ancient Constitution—A Problem in the History of Ideas." *Historical Journal* 3 (1960):125–43. An extremely thoughtful relation of Burke's constitutional thought to the development of the Common Law.

Prior, James. *Memoir of the Life and Character of the Right Hon. Edmund Burke.* London: Baldwin, Cradock, and Joy, 2d ed., 1826. One of the earliest biographies, still of interest.

Smith, Robert A. "Burke's Crusade against the French Revolution: Principles and Prejudices." *Burke Newsletter* 7 (1966):552–69. Maintains that Burke's opposition to the revolution proceeded directly from positions long and consistently held.

Stanlis, Peter J. *Edmund Burke and the Natural Law.* Ann Arbor: University of Michigan Press, 1958. By far the most militant of the natural law interpretations of Burke's thought.

———. "A Preposterous Way of Reasoning: Frederick Dreyer's Edmund Burke: The Philosopher in Action." *Studies in Burke and His Time* 15 (1974):265–75. A thunderbolt hurled in the general direction of Dreyer's attempt to question the natural-law interpretation.

————, ed. *The Relevance of Edmund Burke.* New York: P. J. Kennedy and Sons, 1964. Essays from a symposium by a gathering of Burke's admirers eager to induct him into the twentieth century.

Strauss, Leo. *Natural Right and History.* Chicago: University of Chicago Press, 1953. With Kirk and Hoffmann and Levack, one of the earlier natural-law interpretations of Burke by an eminent political philosopher.

Sutherland, Lucy S. "Edmund Burke and the Relations between Members of Parliament and Their Constituents: An Examination of the Eighteenth-century Theory and Practice in Instructions to Representatives." *Studies in Burke and His Time* 10 (1968):1005–21. Argues that Burke's position vis-à-vis his Bristol constituents was the orthodox one for his time but was coming under challenge from the new urban radicalism.

Underdown, P. T. *Bristol and Burke.* Bristol: Bristol Branch of the Historical Association, 1961. A brief examination of Burke's tenure as representative for that city.

Weston, John C., Jr. "Edmund Burke's View of History." *Review of Politics* 23 (1961):203–29. The most interesting contribution is an analysis of whether or not Burke believed human nature to be static or mutable through history, an issue upon which the author cannot make up his mind.

White, Ian. "The Problem of Burke's Political Philosophy." *Historical Journal* 11 (1968):555–65. A scathing review of Wilkins's book, but valuable for suggestions as to which Burke studies might profitably take.

Wilkins, Burleigh Taylor. *The Problem of Burke's Political Philosophy.* Oxford: Clarendon Press, 1967. An occasionally obscure attempt at a restatement of the natural-law interpretation of Burke.

Index